BLAST OFF

Blast Off

Rapiemur

Till Jesus Shouts

Fourth Edition

Expanded – Including

Jesus Himself Speaks to The Rapture

23 Bible Versions – 900+ Scriptures

1200+ Indexed Scripture References

TL Farley

By TL Farley

4-7-2020

XULON PRESS

Matt. 11:30

Xulon Press
2301 Lucien Way #415
Maitland, FL 32751
407.339.4217
www.xulonpress.com

Printed in the United States of America.
ISBN-13: 978-1-4984-2117-1

Our Pre-Rapture Goal :

but having " ... renounced the hidden things of dishonesty, not walking in craftiness, nor handling the word of God deceitfully; but by manifestation of the truth commending ourselves to every man's conscience in the sight of God." {II Cor. 4:2, KJV}

To become fully alive To Jesus' Imminent Atom-Smashing Shout

On the Day that Must Be called 'Today' !

"... eagerly waiting for the adoption, the redemption of our body. For we were saved in this hope."
{Rom 8:23-24, NKJV}

Jesus: "37 And what I say unto you I say unto all, Watch."
{Mark 13:37; Au-KJV}

"3 Blessed is he that readeth, and they that hear the words of this prophecy, and keep those things which are written therein: for the time is at hand."
{Revelation 1:3, Au-KJV}

Blast Off Rapiemur !

By
TL Farley

...

The Greatest Ride off the Earth !

...

How to Anticipate Divine Ecstasy !

...

An Ancient Mystery Revealed Again !!!
A Biblical Chronology of our Blessed Hope

...

From Genesis To Revelation

A prophecy revealed, taught & fully anticipated

IN

The 1st Century Church

Until

This present hour ...

When Jesus Shouts !

15 Study to shew thyself approved unto God, a workman that needeth not to be ashamed, rightly dividing the word of truth."
{II Timothy 2:15, Au-KJV}

Table of Contents

Dedication to the Church of Philadelphia

---

*"And to the angel of the church in Philadelphia
write; These things saith he that is holy, he that is true,
"he that hath the key of David, he that openeth, and
no man shutteth; and shutteth, and no man openeth;
"I know thy works: behold, I have set before thee an
open door, and no man can shut it: for thou hast
a little strength, and hast kept my word,
and hast not denied my name.
"Behold, I will make them of the synagogue of Satan,
which say they are Jews, and are not, but do lie; behold,
"I will make them to come and worship before thy
feet, and to know that I have loved thee.*

*"<u>Because thou hast kept the word of my patience, I
also will keep thee from the hour of temptation, which
shall come upon all the world,
to try them that dwell upon the earth.
Behold, I come quickly: hold that fast which thou
hast, that no man take thy crown</u>."*

*"Him that overcometh will I make a pillar in the temple
of my God, and he shall go no more out: and I will
write upon him the name of my God, and the name of
the city of my God, which is new Jerusalem, which
cometh down out of heaven from my God: and I will
write upon him my new name. He that hath an ear, let
him hear what the Spirit saith unto the churches."
{Rev. 3:7-13, King James Version}*

The Charge

"I charge you by the Lord that this epistle be read unto all the holy brethren." {The Apostle Paul, I Thessalonians 5:27, KJV}

"But if an unbeliever or an inquirer comes in while everyone is prophesying, they are convicted of sin and are brought under judgment by all, as the secrets of their hearts are laid bare. So they will fall down and worship God, exclaiming, "God is really among you!" {I Corinthians 14:24-25, New International Version}

"For I know that my redeemer liveth, and that he shall stand at the latter day upon the earth..." {Job 19:25, KJV}

"... that man doth not live by bread only, but by every word that proceedeth out of the mouth of the Lord doth man live." {Deuteronomy 8:3d, Authorized KJV}

"... [4] *But he (Jesus) answered and said, "... <u>it is written</u>, Man shall not live by bread alone, but by every word that proceedeth out of the mouth of God."* {Matthew 4:4, Au-KJV}

"For verily I say unto you, till heaven and earth pass, one jot or one tittle shall in no wise pass from the law, till all be fulfilled." {Matt. 5:18, KJV}

"[3] *Call unto me, and I will answer thee, and shew thee great and mighty things, which thou knowest not."* {Jeremiah 33:3, KJV}

Introduction

The Greatest Controversy

"Think not that I am come to send peace on earth: I came not to send peace, but a sword." {Matt. 10:34, KJV}

This was the revelation Jesus spoke to his disciples as He prepared them to go out for the first time to represent Him and proclaim the Gospel of the Kingdom.

Christians, both friend and foe alike can attest to the truth of being confronted with hostility when entering conversations concerning Jesus, the Ha Maschiach, the Jewish Messiah, the Saviour of the world.

In fact, a memorable revelation was shared one morning at a Messianic Congregation gathering. As folks were mingling, saying hello to friends and greeting visitors, one man approached smiling. Taking my hand warmly, he leaned in and whispered in my ear, "Jesus is the hot button!"

Small effort is required to result in verbal fisticuffs simply by stating what one believes and expresses concerning Jesus and His teachings.

In other words, one can focus on a seemingly obscure quote, or instead, upon a major doctrine, and uproot deep-seated antagonisms challenging one's perspective when dealing with Jesus Himself and His words and teachings.

As a young Christian I was always impressed when at the end of a service the men would gather down front to discuss the morning's sermon, which invariably sprouted observations and perspectives from throughout the Bible, ranging from New Testament to Old. This point of considering contentions is brought into sharp relief by noting the name of this congregation, my very first membership, "Way of the Cross Baptist Church."

Perhaps obviously therefore, the more important the teaching, the greater the risk of controversy, and consequently more fervent the immediate, spontaneous interjections, occasionally violently, from all quarters at postulations great and small.

Invariably theological conflicts would arise. Always, each discussion would eventually end when someone finally offered, "Yes, but Jesus said ...".

A quiet would then envelope those joined in, and one by one, conversants would fall to contemplation and drift away.

One would think that this problem would be lessened when one conversed with those in agreement on major events, especially revolving around prophecy. Yet, especially here, even today, seemingly agreeable conversation nose-dives in a heartbeat when one crosses so-called 'orthodox', traditional, accepted understandings of a given future event.

Strangest of all, perhaps, is that a close study of the original writings of the 1st century Church, beginning with Jesus' proclamations, reveal the then 'orthodox' stance on the pre-millennial, pre-Tribulation, imminent, any moment elopement by Jesus with His Bride on a day that *must be called 'today.'*

This 'orthodox' teaching has become over the centuries clouded into obscurity, leaving in its' wake a plethora of positions at this hour proclaiming diametrically opposed stances on the Rapture, its' timing, even to its' reality.

Intentionally, this work shall endeavor to encompass that position which can instantaneously arouse ire against we proponents, we banded few, of this much maligned 'imminent Rapture' position, scheduled to detonate at the atom-splitting shout of Jesus some twinkling-of-an-eye moment 'today.'!!!

In fact, without exaggeration, simply put when considering Biblical prophecy, and in particular, our Blessed Hope, suggesting Jesus Himself speaks to the Rapture may well be the most unnerving and greatest controversy throughout Christian prophetic circles in this moment.

Focusing on the imminent aspect of the prophecy, or 'instantaneity', the core block upon which our Blessed Hope doth stand, as believed to be referenced by Jesus Himself, detonates its' own immediate war. This point is violently objected to even amongst some within Christendom supporting the pre-Tribulation Rapture, even while agreeing with other major tenets of this prophecy.

One may be nonplussed to discover, even though most of the Scriptural verses accepted concerning our Lord's any moment shout to elope with His Bride may be uttered without concern, references and attributions to Jesus Himself speaking to the Rapture can be vociferously objected to, even with undisguised vehemence, and dare one suggest bare-faced 'hostility'? Close relationships founded on fellowshipping over the joyful anticipation of our Lord's expected calling out can in an instant be shattered. This writer, for one, has suffered these sudden abrasions and consequential losses of fellowship.

The good news of His soon-coming, since most holding this prophetic position agree it could not only be tomorrow, but even, may one also suggest 'today itself', demands therefore a more measured consideration of the Gospels, to discern if in fact Jesus made any reference at all to the elopement with His Bride.

Certainly, some would hurry to challenge such a study as unneedful because the time of the trumpet sounding is so near. Others would object the superfluity of such study since the time of His Shout is unknown. Shouldn't all available hands be out beating the bush for that famous final last sheep lost in the wilderness of this world?

Even a cursory inspection of the mission field obligates one to admit, there are in the present-day vernacular 'tons', or if you prefer earlier age language 'scads' of missionary outreaches across the planet, giving their very lives in earnest search for this specific final 'golden fleece'!

This writer discovered how far reaching the mission effort has expanded while visiting in a conference purposed to encourage leaders of dozens of independent mission groups, all vying for the attention of the Body, in hopes of winning support to their hallowed searches for the lost souls of planet earth.

Entering for lunch into a large cafeteria-style gathering, a lone disciple was spotted at a table with no joiners. Getting a plate of food, it was decided by this participant to join said figure in hopes of encouraging him in his vision. After introductions were made, we quickly settled into our plates, each of us visiting with the purpose of finding out who the other guy was. It was learned the lone fellow was in fact the founder of an outreach on a foreign continent, whose plan was to target the leaders of the various countries, bringing them to the Lord, and thereby changing the eternal destinies of said countries, and the millions of inhabiting souls.

At once overwhelmed by the immensity of this man's massive commitment, this servant immediately volunteered to join up and help on the front lines of this towering task.

Not missing a stroke of his fork gathering food from the plate, the man in quest of a continent replied blithely, with a hint of bored disinterest, "No thanks, I've got all the help I need."

Unscathed by the rebuff, still in earnest desire to comfort and strengthen a brother, I rejoindered joyfully, "Praise the Lord!"

Taken aback and visibly confused by my exuberant reception of his rejection he could only reply through his mouthful of lunch, "What?"

Motioning to the scores of overflowing tables of missionaries around us, at which vibrant discussions were in play, I explained, "I've been doing mission work for over 15 years, and I'll bet if I went around this room, I wouldn't find another mission group that had all the folks they needed to help!"

It seemed a cooling fell over our table and we both finished our meals in contemplation.

Martyring is rising across the world. Troubles, trials and tribulations are proliferating exponentially, in the midst of the multiplied, frenetic activities to be about the Father's business across the planet.

Rising above the din of calls to salvation before Jesus elopes with His Bride in a Shout remains the divisive challenge: Did Jesus Himself actually speak to the Rapture? Specifically did Jesus speak to its' 'imminence'?

Let's take a look.
Foreword

Now Boarding!!!

Destination: The Greatest Ride off Earth!

Anticipation

P erhaps one of the most exciting moments for a trav-
eler are the blaring announcements over the public
address system, "Now Boarding! Now Boarding!"
Consider in the place of these stirring announcements
Paul's continuing declarations that Jesus will herald His
eloping with His Bride with a 'Shout'!

As He descends down through the heavens to above
the earth, Jesus will Shout for His Bride, the Church,
calling her up to His side! Just one.

When? That 'Shout' is imminent! Any moment on
that day called 'today'. Wherever you are at the moment
of that shout will be your launching pad!

Ready or not!

Even for those naturally impatient for an ending, this
moment shall be astonishingly brief, so please allow
me to retrace the salient point of this book, which is the

atom-smashing, any moment Shout of Jesus to elope with His Bride, the Church, on a day that must be called 'today'!

Many are at least somewhat aware of prophecies related to what are euphemistically called 'the end times.' (In other words, 'the bridge is out!')

Headlines shout across the psyche daily from an unending torrent of media outlets shocking the sensibilities, led by such Biblical gems as "Anti-Christ", "Tribulation", "End of the World," and trailing somewhat behind as a good step-child should, shrouded in proper skepticism, the also-ran popularly known as "the Rapture."

Aware of the scores of films, tv specials, conferences, books, websites and watch-groups proliferating the excesses of highlighting Jesus' Shout for His Bride, etc., that pay tribute to this doctrine, a reality must first be documented. Even many of the major stars of the most successful films on the Rapture don't really believe in our Blessed Hope! Nicholas Cage famously remarked, when asked why he was doing a movie about the Rapture, "... because I never really thought about it." Good choice, Nick! Perfect time to consider prophecy!

These varied futuristic perspectives are of course all within the Christian realm.

Christian Bibles, of which there are over 900 translations, not to mention additional literary formats, encompass these flashpoint terms, such as 'end times', with varying degrees of attention. A myriad of other submissions from various religious and secular approaches may be included here, though the title of this work gives way to the focused area of study at the apex of Church history. (Pun intended)

Narrowing the field then, one captures a sterling reality upon inspection of the days in which Biblical history is proffered to culminate. Of the two main topics vying for first look, the anti-Christ/Tribulation/One-World-Government appears at least a good length or two ahead of the other, more mysterious, plainly derided proclamation popularly known as 'the Rapture.'

Yet, there is one aspect which divides the two prophetical areas of consideration by an even greater margin, a good country mile. Where there is no teaching anywhere in all of Scripture as to the exact timing or appearance of the anti-Christ, conversely the Rapture, each Christian's 'Blessed Hope', is startlingly couched and presented, encouraged and forewarned of, to be kept in a Christian's daily walk as pre-eminently imminent. And this was the practice of the first-generation church, as shall be exemplified authoritatively by Scripture itself.

Yes, the Tribulation, of which some even demand is in fact now operating, (which it is not), is never once in all of Holy Writ, ever, ever encouraged to be ANTICIPATED ! To be feared, avoided at all costs, yes! But nowhere in the Bible is the Tribulation prophesied to be IMMINENT! Scripture clearly and plainly prophesies the Tribulation will be seen approaching from the horizon!

The Rapture, our 'rapiemur', conversely is continually posited as about to happen at any moment on a day that MUST be called 'today'! Putting our Blessed Hope doctrine clearly as far ahead of all other end-time proclamations as Secretariat blasting to the 1973 Belmont Stakes Crown 31 lengths ahead of the nearest nose of clueless nags, capturing the legendary Triple Crown !!! {See the film 'Secretariat'!}

This being true, how then does the individual believer incorporate this reality into his or her everyday walk !?!?!?

Let's take a further look …

As a young boy, beginning as I remember when I was roughly five or six years old, adults often asked me what I was going to be when I grew up. And I would proudly reply, "A train conductor!"

Mostly people would respond with delighted laughter and go on. But occasionally curiosity would arouse the questioner to probe, "Really? A train conductor, why is that?" My response would be, "Well, then I could travel on a train and take people's tickets. I could talk to them and find out where they are going."

My Aunt Gert used to take my brothers and me on train trips every year into Chicago. Watching the train conductors was fascinating, as they passed through the coach, punching tickets and talking to people. That seemed to me the most glorious job in the world. To be able to talk to people about who they were, and where they were traveling to, all the while discovering the different places to go in the world.

On occasion there would be someone who had boarded the train in a hurry without paying. The conductor would then pull out a wad of tickets and the passenger would buy one. Then the conductor would punch the ticket, to show the person was all set to ride to their destination and everything would be just fine.

Now remind yourself that you are here at the very edge of the future and eternity.

A delightful example of the imminent Rapture actually happening comes in the final scene of the movie "Matrix," when 'Neo,' portrayed excellently by Keanu Reeves, steps into an outdoor public phone booth in a metropolitan city and begins to speak into the phone. "We know you are out there," he declares. Then he begins to describe a world available to any who are searching for something greater than their present reality. He invites any that are listening to join him.

Hanging up, Neo steps from the booth and blasts off into the sky!

Writing this book about the imminent Rapture has been a real joy but I would be terribly remiss in the telling if I neglected the most important part of the purpose of sharing this information with each reader. And that is to ensure that all accepting this looming prophecy are themselves set to be raptured. Two questions will suffice for confirmation.

Get Your Ticket!!

First, do you have your ticket?

You, the reader, may have already been wondering 'what about a ticket'?

Obviously, in order to get your ticket punched, you must first possess a ticket. Notice I didn't say you must first 'buy' a ticket. The reason being there are no tickets for sale. So, again, do you, the reader, <u>have</u> a ticket?

There are, of course, no real tickets to Heaven for sale. That doesn't mean people aren't on the street, holding rallies, producing TV specials, and using the internet in order to offer false tickets for sale. So, how can you be sure the ticket you possess is real and not false? The fact that it is going to cost you something proves it is false.

Jesus' Omega Word!

Jesus called out at the moment of His death, "Tetelestai."

John 19:30 reads, "When Jesus had received the sour wine, he said, 'It is finished', and he bowed his head and gave up his spirit." {ESV}

This word 'tetelestai' that Jesus used was a common Greek term in the marketplaces of His day. Greek being the *'Lingua Franca'* of that time, (the 'language of money' developed to transact business in the market-places of the world among those whose native languages are different at the completion of the transaction, when full payment is made.) When a transaction was agreed upon and the full sum accounted was paid to the seller, a document could be produced that was stamped with this word, 'tetelestai,' as a bill of sale for the business just completed, verifying the buyer had 'paid' the cost of the item in question. *Strong's Exhaustive Concordance of the Bible* defines the root word *'teleo'* as: "… complete, execute, conclude, discharge (a debt)."

So why *'tetelestai'*? It is the passive, past tense of the verb *'teleo'*, clarifying the action as *'has been accomplished'*. What, you might ask, has been accomplished/ paid for? The sins of the whole world were atoned for by Jesus' death on the cross.' His staying dead was impossible for He is the Son of God, the second person of the Trinity.

Therefore, Jesus Himself pronounced the debt of sin for all mankind for all of history as being *'paid in full'* by His death. Hence, 'tetelestai'. He declared, "It is finished." To prove the payment good, three days later Jesus arose from the dead.

And now Jesus stands at the heart's door of each and every boy, girl, man and woman on earth that does not yet know Him. In the person of the Holy Spirit He knocks, inviting all who answer to receive Him as Lord and Savior. Anyone who hears His voice and opens the door, Jesus will enter unto them. "And whosoever calls upon the name of the Lord shall be saved." {Rom. 10:13; Rev. 3:20; Jerimiah 33:3}

It was my joy over 40 years ago to pray to Jesus. I told Him that I had always thought I knew Him. I had told my sins to other men who were to take my sins to God. But now, in this book I was reading, "The Late Great Planet Earth", I discovered how I could know for certain personally that I was going to Heaven.

I had been taught, and this teaching continues to this day, that a person commits the sin of presumption when declaring they know for certain they are going to Heaven.

Yet, reading I John 5:13, discovering that the Bible was written specifically so that a person is able (should know in this present moment) for certain they were going to Heaven, was mind boggling. That they might know it in their present, conscious state; additionally, inspiring them to continue to believe and follow in Jesus.

If you call, Jesus will answer. You must repent of your sin, of course. Establishing your guilt is easy. Have you ever lusted for anything or anyone? Guilty. Jesus said to look on a woman with lust is committing adultery in your heart. Have you ever desired anything belonging to anyone else? That is the sin of coveting. Guilty. Have you ever been angry with anyone? Guilty before God. Jesus said if we just get angry with someone we have already committed murder in our hearts in God's eyes.

Knowing you are a sinner allows you to seek God's mercy. Jesus told of a man in the temple that could not even lift his eyes to heaven that prayed, 'God, have mercy on me a sinner.' Jesus said that man went down to his house justified before God. {Luke 18:13, NIV}

Jesus said if a person is guilty of the smallest sin that person is guilty before God of all sins. Paul wrote, "For all have sinned and come short of the Glory of God." Paul said that there is no one who is righteous in the world. None. {Rom. 3:10 & 23, KJV}

The knowledge that you are a sinner is a blessing. Why? That simply means you can now confess to Jesus that you *are* a sinner. Ask Him to save you. Jesus said to ask, and you will receive.

To ensure that everyone on the earth has access to this eternal gift of salvation that is already paid for, the apostle Paul was inspired to write Romans 10:13, "For everyone who calls on the name of the Lord will be saved." {Holman Christian Standard Bible}

Therefore, each person is qualified to call on Jesus for salvation. And God adds an additional refinement that clarifies the assurance of salvation provided by Jesus' atoning death to all who call upon Him through the entire explanatory passage of Rom. 10:9-13:

"If you confess with your mouth, 'Jesus is Lord,' and believe in your heart that God raised Him from the dead, you will be saved. One believes with the heart, resulting in righteousness, and one confesses with the mouth, resulting in salvation. Now the Scripture says, everyone who believes on Him will not be put to shame, for there is no distinction between Jew and Greek, since the same

Lord of all is rich to all who call on Him. For everyone who calls on the name of the Lord will be saved." {HCSB}

Make certain you have your ticket to ride. Call on Jesus. Confess that you are a sinner in need of His forgiveness. Plead His Blood, shed on the cross for you and me personally, as payment. Believe in your heart that Jesus is Lord and that God raised Him from the dead. Jesus is rich in mercy. You will be saved. Begin with any one of these steps and He will lead you. You may even pray the prayer of the man who cried to Jesus, "...I do believe, but help me overcome my unbelief!" {Mark 9:24, New Living Translation}

As simple as this sounds, remember Jesus said, "... and my yoke is easy, my burden is light." And for a guarantee that your prayer is accepted right now by God who hears, the Apostle John wrote, "These things have I written unto you that believe on the name of the Son of God; that ye may know that ye have eternal life, and that ye may believe on the name of the Son of God." {Matt. 11:30; I John 5:13; KJV}

'...That you may know that you have eternal life, and that you may believe on the name of the Son of God.'

If I may repeat for emphasis, I John 5:13 was the verse that caused me to realize that God wanted even me to personally know for certain that I have, present tense, eternal life in Him. That was 45 years ago, September 22, 1974.

God has made many more sure words of prophecy plain to me over these continuing decades. And they always humble me to realize how much more there is to learn. Especially with God, the more you know the more you know you don't know!

But I now have the confidence to know that I have eternity in which to learn all I desire to know.

Anticipate !!!

Second, has your ticket been punched? "For it is by believing in your heart that you are made right with God, and it is by confessing with your mouth that you are saved." If you believe in Jesus in your heart God counts your belief as righteousness before Him. {Rom. 10:10, NLT}

Your telling people of your faith in Jesus is what confirms your salvation to God. "Has the LORD redeemed you? Then speak out! Tell others he has redeemed you from your enemies." {Psalm 107:2, NLT}

Now you're in the game. The next major, divine event on the schedule will spring from the atom-smashing Shout of Jesus, inside 11/100th's of a second in which an eye instantaneously twinkles, is the imminent, any moment Rapture! And you will be reading in the following pages how the first believers taught and anticipated the Shout of Jesus at any moment in each day!

If you have prayed this prayer, or you already know Jesus, then you have an eternal ticket to the greatest ride off earth. And you won't have to lift a finger to get on the ride. You are going to be ecstatically, violently snatched away by **His love,** in a moment, in the twinkling of an eye, while it is still called 'today.'

And as all of Jesus' prophecies concerning the end of this age continue to exponentially converge upon each other, look up with anticipation and listen for His Shout!

Be ready for a jolt of Divine Ecstasy! Join with the rest of us, as we pray:

Thy Kingdom come, even so, Lord Jesus!

Polishing the Brass Ring

To emphasize the point, please remember, Paul promised a crown to '...all who <u>eagerly</u> look forward to **his** appearing....'

If everyone going in the Rapture was going to be awarded a crown, even those not looking for and anticipating His calling out, what would be the point in awarding that crown, let alone striving to win the race?

There would be no *raison d'être (...the most important reason or purpose for someone or something's existence ...)* for giving out a crown! {II Timothy 4:8, NLT}

Till the Shout!!!

Chapter One

The Rapture Is 'Today'

———————◦———————

Recent decades have seen an increasing undulation of temperatures, and weather changing the times and seasons across America and even the world. These temperature and consequential weather pattern oscillations first gave impetus to warnings of 'global warming'. God explains, "He changes the times and seasons…" {Daniel 2:21, HCSB}

To what purpose has God been changing the seasons in and out and up and down? Some have even begun to question whether these dramatic weather yaws are signs of the end of this age, or, even the end of this world.

Has the world entered upon its last days? Is the end of the world really approaching? Really? Is it coming soon? How soon? Who says? What about the Four Blood Moons? Where is America in prophecy? For that matter, what is the world's future in general? Specifically, what about the often-touted Christian claim, the Rapture of the Church?

Is Jesus really going to evacuate His Bride before the Tribulation begins? Is He going to snatch the Church out of this world before the global trials befall the earth and its populations? Is it truly going to happen at <u>*any moment*</u> on a day called 'today'? Has the Bible alluded to the imminent Rapture from the beginning of the Church age?

Great interest was stirred in recent years concerning the signs of the four blood moons. Many studies have brought prominence to prophetic verses relating to end time events. Interest even proliferated ongoing public discussion of America's continuance as a nation. Escalating political strife and economic woes each lend themselves to prophesied scenarios.

At a Bible study on the book of Revelation, a man presented the teacher with a flurry of questions challenging the authenticity of the Bible.

Following the meeting I approached the gentleman to suggest he read Lee Strobel's book, "The Case for the Real Jesus," which deals with many of the questions he was posing. He immediately recognized Strobel's work, declaring he loved and had read all of Strobel's books.

As our conversation broadened I discovered he was a practicing lawyer and has been a law Professor at a leading American university for over four decades. When I repeated for him the title of the suggested book, he was taken aback, and admitted he'd never heard that specific title. This memo-missing surprise is a common response due to Strobel's prolific writing and voluminous media output.

Intelligent, articulate, even brilliantly bright, the lawyer seemed well-rounded in his own study, equipped to consider any topic at hand. My amazement at his exposure to so many fields of inquiry was profoundly jolted when I learned he had no apparent interest in examining prophecy. He admitted it 'just didn't excite him very much.'

My astonishment at his admitted lack of zeal for prophecy was heightened by his readiness to discuss Jesus and the Bible with obvious zest. Yet the Bible includes the proclamation, "...*For the testimony of Jesus is the spirit of prophecy*." {Revelation 19:10, ESV}

Thus, the more deeply involved one becomes in the sayings of Jesus, the more one is exposed to the prophecies of God.

Disinterest in prophecy becomes understandable when confronted with the often-conflicting prophetical views of Christians. This holds true especially among those in leadership, in particular concerning the imminent Rapture.

A noted Bible teacher replete with national media connections, also bearing international acclaim from Christian leaders, described his own belief in the imminent Rapture.

The acclaimed scholar coupled Jesus' any-moment calling out of His Bride with the statement of apparent conviction the event may not deploy *for another three thousand years*!

If that great a span of time may be considered in estimating the fulfillment of the imminent Rapture, surely the gate is wide open to increase the margin. Perhaps our Blessed Hope won't erupt for 10,000 years. etc., etc., etc.

More surprisingly, this same teacher also suggested the Jews might be brought back into the land several more times before Bible proclamation of their return to Israel is fulfilled prophetically.

Most intriguingly, challenged with the position that the any-moment Rapture of the Bride of Messiah *is* imminent, that same teacher confided privately he himself believes in the imminence!

His closing heartfelt prayer for the session, before this disclosure was made, proclaimed his hope of this event '...while it is called 'today.' Surely, within this wide-ranging view of 'from any moment today to 3,000 years hence,' a more clearly defined window can be made for believers to watch for the Rapture.

One can only commiserate with the lawyer who, due to such vague parameters for this event being proclaimed, found his interest in prophecy difficult to muster.

When one wonders at the depth of revelation God bestows on believers, Isaiah's sermon instructions from God come to mind revealing His command for unbelievers:

> *"He (God) said, 'Go and tell this people: Be ever hearing, but never understanding; be ever seeing, but never perceiving. Make the heart of this people calloused; make their ears dull and close their eyes. Otherwise they might see with their eyes, hear with their ears, understand with their hearts, and turn and be healed.'" {Isaiah 6:9-10, NIV}*

Christians, even so, though agreeing on so much, still differ widely on many issues, per example the timed execution of the Rapture. How does one establish a correct attitude to the imminent Rapture? By taking heed unto His Word.

One clue is given when Jesus opens God's instructions to Isaiah while explaining the purpose of parables to the disciples, "He replied, 'Because the knowledge of the secrets of the kingdom of heaven has been given to you, but not to them.'" Joined with Paul's admission that now we only know in part, one understands particulars on prophecies shall continue to be refined and clarified right up to the Shout. This definition, according to the verses just quoted, shall only be made available to willing believers. {Isaiah 6:9; Matthew 13:11; NIV}

The lawyer's view of prophecy as a seemingly boorish subject is understandable. Believers have been given the prescribed span of time for the ignition of the Rapture as 'from any moment now to thousands of years from today.' By quoting believing scholars such as the renowned teacher just referenced, the acceptable attitude towards anticipating the calling out seems to be unimportant. A shortcoming becomes apparent when increasing the waiting time of fulfillment which erases the teaching of imminence.

Most people are familiar with amusement parks and the rides that are offered for entertainment and excitement. Permit the roller coaster to pop into your mind as an example. There are admittedly today scads more rides with greater degrees of challenge, but the roller coaster will do for example.

At this writing there are companies now selling tickets for rides out to the edges of space beyond earth's atmosphere. Other enterprises are advertising preparation for rides to the Moon, Mars and beyond! Our focus, however, is not on distance, but on the launch itself.

Whatever ride you can envision, there is a Biblical prophecy of a heavenly launch that is approaching the populations of the earth which shall eclipse completely any ride that shall ever be invented on this planet. Clearly, many of these rides are in the preparatory stage, which eliminates them from the imminent possibility. And the further removed their implementation, the more impossible to associate such plans with imminence.

Suggesting the Rapture could happen in 3,000 years erases the very possibility of imminence. This suggestion of a distant Rapture puts at immediate risk multitudes of those who could miss what can easily be billed as the 'Greatest Ride off the Earth.' Who after all, prepares for events in future millenniums?

An even greater risk is accepted when one allows for ignoring the certainties of Scripture, as our scholar, who though professing belief in imminence, allows for a disheveling projection of expanding time instead of a firm lock on imminent anticipation.

Lest you relegate this last statement to exaggeration, allow me to offer a brief description of what is coming.

According to prophetic scripture, specifically Rapture-related, much of which shall be examined in this book, there is a deliverance coming for all believers in Jesus, grave-ensconced first, immediately followed by 'we who are alive and remain,' from the increasing terrors of this present age. Believers are instructed to 'anticipate' this 'escape'. But laying the disobedience of that encouragement aside, let us consider a greater mishap. {I Thess. 4:17}

That deliverance shall be a lovingly violent, individual, personal snatching up and away to the heavens in a moment, in the twinkling of an eye, of each and every believer by Jesus Christ, the Messiah of Israel, faster than you the reader or I can imagine this phenomenon. It has been suggested that if one tries to think about the Rapture itself, the event has already passed. It is going to be that quick!

Where are all the Christians going? To be with Jesus.

Again, emphasis intended, this ecstatic snatching away can easily, *sans* any exaggeration, be best described and even billed as 'The Greatest Ride off the Earth.' And you won't need a space suit as you rocket out of this galaxy!

In fact, the most complete definition of the English phrase rendered from the Latin for this prophecy would more properly be 'violently' ecstatic. Which leads one who adheres to II Timothy 3:16, and the divine inspiration of all Scripture, to interpret the fulfillment of the term in question, 'rapiemur', as Divine *'violence.'*

Presently, many Christians are awaiting that launch, which is proclaimed to be scheduled for any moment in the time frame designated as 'today.' Thus, the prophecy is preached as being 'imminent.'

The revered teacher noted earlier is counting himself among believers looking for this calling out at any moment. The problem remains: His conclusion that the event could possibly take another 3,000 years to employ opens the door to possibilities of even longer or shorter gestation periods before the climax of this 'twinkling of an eye' he is suggesting.

Setting aside momentarily the spiritual whiplash that would occur should the Shout erupt sooner than later for those of his postulation, a stickier problem arises.

Multitudes are already rejecting Jesus' offer of salvation and consequential deliverance. The lengthening of Rapture detonation time encourages the uncommitted to continue delaying any decisions related to God.

Many passages throughout Scripture, beginning in the Old Testament, warn against putting off making decisions in regard to the Lord. Jeremiah 8:20 reveals, "Harvest is past, summer is ended, and we are not saved." Hebrews 3:15 warns, "...As it is said, *'TODAY* IF YOU HEAR

HIS VOICE, DO NOT HARDEN YOUR HEARTS, AS WHEN THEY PROVOKED ME.'" {NASB; Au-KJV}

Jesus Himself is famously quoted in the Sermon on the Mount, Matt. 6:34, "Take therefore no thought for the morrow:" Certainly the Lord is instructing against borrowing worries from the future. But within the statement is the realization one must stay focused on the here and now of each present day we are in. {KJV}

For example, shouldn't one be more concerned with this life first? How, per example, is one going to eat, where is one going to live, and what is one going to wear? These are important concerns, though only scratching the surface of the continuing daily needs of one's life.

And, these are the very issues Jesus teaches in the Sermon on the Mount that we should defer to the most important issue, seeking the Kingdom of God first.

Also, thinking gains clarity when one begins to focus on coming events that are nearer. What are the possible major happenings for the near future? What could the next year bring? Are there any special events coming down the pike that could be scintillating to anticipate? Is there any important, life-changing, destiny-catapulting prophecy scheduled for any moment this day we are now in? Is there _anything_ that could happen today?

Only one major prophecy available to the population of the entire earth could happen today at any moment. All other major prophecies are set in their time and place.

Multitudes across the world think nothing of traveling great distances to afford them the opportunity to stand in long lines, sometimes for hours, in order to spend a few, brief moments on exhilarating rides of thrill-convulsing proportions. Great patience must be exercised by the throngs as they inch towards the front of the queue and their moment with temporal exhilaration.

But even this analogy is limited. Here are some important differences. Other than the trumpet there will be no other sound in the exercise of this prophecy. Christians in line for the Rapture will not take their turn to mount a machine to ride. In a literal atom-smashing moment, inside the twinkling of an eye, which encompasses $11/100^{th}$'s of a second, masses from graves across the earth and sea will instantaneously have their mortal forms changed to immortality while being simultaneously catapulted into the heavens. Inside that same $11/100^{th}$'s of a second, **all Christians** who are alive and remain on this earth shall be 'caught away' in simultaneous, instantaneous change to incorruptible immortality, ever to be with Jesus!

Interestingly, those who are dead, whose spirits are with Jesus shall not experience this event in the same way we who are yet alive and remain.

A wonderful definition for 'rapture' fielded from the internet:
A feeling of intense pleasure and joy:

Synonyms:
Ecstasy, bliss, euphoria, elation, exaltation, joyfulness, cloud nine, seventh heaven, transport, rhapsody, enchantment, exhilaration, happiness, pleasure, ravishment, top of the world; (as in) 'delectation': enjoyment, gratification, delight,; (to include) expressions of intense pleasure and enthusiasm ...

By these standards it is obvious that we are not exaggerating or employing hyperbole!

As one who believes, contemplates, and strives to anticipate this miraculous experience, the expectation of this divine moment can only be described as 'Divine ecstasy.'

Rushing down upon humanity is a prophecy fulfillment that any on earth would give their life and fortune to participate in because it shall be without parallel both the most spectacular physical, and spiritual experience that shall ever be this side of Heaven. Stunningly, the event itself is merely the beginning of eternity with God.

So, we wait daily, moment to moment, for that lovingly violent, snatching away, doodling along here in life's line, occupying ourselves with the comparatively mundane activities of temporal life. Meanwhile, why not take some time to weigh our understanding of this prophesied 'blast off' that is preached by the Apostle Paul as a 'mystery' told?

Cultivating our understanding of the imminent Rapture shall, in the words of Paul, "comfort and strengthen" each of us that we may better enjoy, and serve, in the time remaining.

This revelation from the Word of God, properly framed and delivered, easily encourages Christians to be anticipating the Rapture 'today.'!

And Blast Off can rightly be shouted to the world as the imminent, any-moment, 'Greatest Ride on Earth!' Popcorn anyone?

{Note: Readers are requested to keep in mind Hebrews 12:1a, "Wherefore seeing we also are compassed about with so great a cloud of witnesses..." to better understand the author presenting his address as to larger audiences than may be readily apparent.} {KJV}

Chapter Two

Jesus Is at the Door

Anticipate His shout at any moment!

Luke 12:45 – "But and if that servant say in his heart, my lord delayeth his coming; and shall begin to beat the menservants and maidens, and to eat and drink, and to be drunken…" {KJV}

Romans 13:12 – "The night is far spent; the day is at hand: let us therefore cast off the works of darkness and let us put on the armour of light." {KJV}

Romans 16:25-26 – "Now to **him** who is able to strengthen you according to my gospel and the preaching of Jesus Christ, according to the revelation of the mystery that was kept secret for long ages but has now been disclosed and through the prophetic writings has been made known to all nations, according to the command of the eternal God, to bring about the obedience of faith…" {ESV}

I Corinthians 15:51-52 – "Listen, I tell you a mystery: We will not all sleep, but we will all be changed — in a flash, in the twinkling of an eye, at the last trumpet. For the trumpet will sound, the dead will be raised imperishable, and we will be changed." {NIV}

Ephesians 1:9 – "Having made known unto us the mystery of **his** will, according to **his** good pleasure which **he** hath purposed in **himself**: {KJV}

"for the administration of the days of fulfillment – to bring everything together in the Messiah, both things in heaven and things on earth in Him." {Eph. 1:10–HCSB}

Hebrews 11:5-6 – "By faith Enoch was translated that he should not see death; and was not found, because God had translated him: for before his translation he had this testimony, that he pleased God. But without faith it is impossible to please **him**: for he that cometh to God must believe that **he** is, and that **he** is a rewarder of them that diligently seek **him**." {KJV}

Revelation 3:20 – "Here I am! I stand at the door and knock. If anyone hears **my** voice and opens the door, I will come in and eat with that person, and they with **me**." {NIV}

Can You Hear Him Knocking?

As a boy working summers in the corn and bean fields of northern Illinois from sun-up to dark-thirty, the end of the day was often too far away to inspire comforting thoughts. But as we worked detasselling, rogueing and hoeing, the end of every other row promised the respite of a refreshing drink of cold water. That was at least enough hope to keep us going down each row toward sundown. Very subtly it was also developing patience.

Hal Lindsey, prolific author, preacher, missionary and prophetic end-times online watchman on the wall to the world, has been quoted as saying, "Man can live about forty days without food, about three days without water, about eight minutes without air...but only for one second without hope." {goodreads.com}

Today shocking events continue to exponentially befall the world, be they local, national, or international. They are evidenced as wars, rumors of wars, terrorism, earthquakes, famines, pestilence, tornadoes and personal tragedies. These thoughts of the promised end of the age and Jesus' Triumphal Return increase as trials intensify with turmoil.

John 14:1-3 dispels troubling moments as we remember Jesus uplifting Peter during the last supper with, "Do not let your heart be troubled...I will come again and receive you to **myself**..." It is no coincidence that Jesus was here speaking of the imminent Rapture. {NASB}

This book is a study of the imminent or any moment 'snatching away' of the Bride of Jesus during the time that is called 'today.' This is by no means an exhaustive study, though exhaustion has often been the result in compiling this work.

Daily continued study invariably unveils new, fruitful and exciting elements of the teaching of Our Blessed Hope. We shall be endeavoring to examine the Rapture from oft-overlooked aspects that coalesce the teachings of our elopement into a more harmonious and certain narrative.

Many suggest this promise in John 14:3 is speaking of the Return of Jesus to earth rather than the controversial and much debated doctrine of the Rapture. Many in Christendom consider these two concepts to be in fact one and the same event.

Was this the first time Jesus spoke of such a promise? Are there references anywhere else in the Bible, either the Old Testament, known to Jewish believers as the Tanakh, or the New Testament, referred to in the Hebrew language as the Brit Chadashah?

Most Christians that accept the doctrine of 'Our Blessed Hope,' identified by many as 'the Rapture,' understand the prophecy is an event without an exact designated time for fulfillment. In other words, though there are Christians who acknowledge a belief in our Blessed Hope as proclaimed by the apostle Paul, most of these believe '*the* moment' of the event is unknowable.

After all, 'no man knows the day or the hour,' is the famous quote declared by Jesus Himself. It is even often contended that contemplating and/or studying this topic is a waste of time. But at the very least, Jesus and several disciples instructed believers not merely to watch for and be expecting Jesus to return, but to actually be anticipating His shout, and to be fortified with the understanding that the event would take place at any moment in the present 'day' in which they were living.

How in the world does one 'anticipate' an event slated for an atom-smashing moment, inside the twinkling of an eye, clocked at 11/100th's of a second, on a day that must be called 'today', not knowing the hour or even the day of execution?

According to many modern teachers, the claim of complete ignorance as to the timing of Jesus' return was the understanding and practice maintained by first-century believers. This accepted interpretation contradicts the Word of God as preached by Jesus, and the Apostles Paul, James, Peter, John and Jude. Further, it contradicts the written word that has come down to us in this present day, exemplified in the practice of those first-generation believers recorded by Paul and others, even commending them for their walk of waiting daily for this event.

Moreover, today we would be in error to merely watch for the end of the age as commanded. Were there no parameters set to identify the time in which the imminent Rapture would be recognizably pending, we would also grow weary anticipating this Blessed event as instructed by John in I John 3:3. Instead, Jesus fore-warned we should be first watching for the signs of the beginning of these turmoil's, bringing us into the season which would herald the entrance of the time of the imminent elopement of the Bride!

This author as well as many others throughout the Body of Messiah believe scripture reveals the world has entered this time of the imminent or any moment Rapture. Further, this anticipation is providing a most intended refreshing and strengthening for these days leading to Jesus catching away His Bride!

Futurist Christians, those staunchly pre-millennial, pre-tribulation, imminent Rapture pro-claimers, believe the world is now in the days just prior to the Tribulation. Christians that have accepted the teaching of the Blessed Hope, acknowledge that the 'any moment' calling out by Jesus is exponentially approaching, moment by moment.

Futurist belief is that 'now' are the days in which every moment of each succeeding day heralds the approaching _blast off_. The 'any moment' calling out proclaimed by Paul is now more obviously 'imminent.' But we shall also consider passages that show the church has been in this anticipatory posture from its beginning.

Per example, Jesus commanded believers, in Luke 21:36, to 'watch' for His calling out that we may 'escape' all the trials that will come upon the earth during the

Tribulation. This exercise of 'watching' will be examined scripturally in the pages to follow.

Still, this author concedes the majority of those in the world who proclaim Jesus as their personal Lord and Savior hold different interpretations of this prophecy. The late Dr. John Walvoord, former Dallas Theological Seminary Chancellor Emeritus, respected during his life by many Bible prophecy scholars across the world as the 'Dean of Bible Prophecy,' thought as much.

Dr. Walvoord recorded this view in the introduction to his monumental work, 'All the Prophecies of the Bible.' He contended that the vast majority of Christendom was uncommitted to this belief in the Rapture. Even so, from his vantage point he not only supported this teaching but promoted it his entire academic life. {Endnotes: *When Now Becomes Too Late*, Chapter I, Note 3, pg. 85}

Alternate perceptions have over the centuries permeated Christendom to such a depth that for the larger percentage in the Body today one popular collective thought has become: the Rapture, if indeed there is one, shall come somewhere near the end of time. And since no man 'knows the day or the hour' believers need not be concerned about the execution or timing of the Rapture.

Only a comparatively small percentage throughout the body of Christendom, which number includes this author and Dr. Walvoord, promote the pre-millennial, pre-Tribulation, imminent, hence any-moment, 'catching' away of the Bride of Messiah. Those of us holding this prophetical stance are self-described 'futurists.'

As mentioned, Acts 1:6-7, perhaps the most oft misapplied passage regarding the 'when' of the Rapture, was Jesus' response to the apostles' question, "Lord, will you at this time restore the kingdom to Israel?" The apostles were actually inquiring as to the time when Jesus would *restore the kingdom to Israel,* which can be readily seen as a completely separate event from the deliverance of *calling out the Bride of Messiah, the Church.* Yet, His response is often quoted as speaking to the Blessed Hope of Christians.

Jesus immediately answered their question by explaining, "It is not for you to know times or seasons, (re: concerning the restoration of the Kingdom to Israel)." He was replying to their query concerning the restoration of the Kingdom to Israel, not referring to the Rapture which the apostles were not inquiring about. So, quoting this passage in connection with the Rapture is in fact misapplying it and taking the verse completely out of context.

Jesus had gathered the apostles on Mount Olivet, "...a Sabbath day's walk" from Jerusalem. He had been giving these followers commandments and instructions throughout his ministry, including the forty days following His resurrection, in preparation of His return to Heaven. Jesus had "shewed Himself alive after His passion by many infallible proofs...speaking of the things pertaining to the kingdom of God..." {Acts 1:12, NIV; 1:3, KJV}

Other misapplications include connecting Jesus' response concerning the restoration of the 'kingdom to Israel' to the promise of 'Our Blessed Hope' in Titus 2:13: "...looking for the blessed hope and glorious appearing of our great God and Savior Jesus Christ." And also misapplying Jesus' '...appearing...' proclaimed in the Titus verse as reference to our Lord's return to earth as specifically described in Rev. 19:11-21 to end the Tribulation. {KJV}

These misconstruances reveal how easily one may wrongly divide the word of truth. Plainly put, Jesus has not yet restored the kingdom to Israel. Although Israel has not only been reinstated (pun intentional) as of May 14, 1948, the nationals continue as a people to converge on *Eretz Israel,* the land given to the Jews by God. Nor shall the kingdom be restored to Israel at the calling out of the Bride of Messiah, not even immediately following this most spectacular fulfillment of prophecy.

The kingdom will only be restored to Israel following the seven-year Tribulation at Jesus' Return to earth, after Jesus separates the sheep from the goats and leads the sheep into the millennium for His thousand-year reign in Jerusalem. In the interest of avoiding too great a digression, the author begs to abstain from considering further any other prophesied fulfillments of that time.

Again, this restoration of the kingdom to the Israelites is enacted following Jesus' return to earth at the end of the Tribulation prior to the beginning of the Millennium, "Then shall the King say unto them on his right hand, come, ye blessed of my Father, inherit the kingdom prepared for you from the foundation of the world..." {Matt. 25:34, Jubilee Bible 2000}

First and Second Watch

God's command for the First Watch in scripture pointed to the Messiah's birth, per Micah 5:2. God's command, Luke 21:36, for a Second Watch points to Messiah calling out his Bride at the imminent Rapture.

Jesus' declaration, Matt. 24:30, ends the Third Watch for the Messiah's return to earth with his Bride and armies.

The term 'watch' is used often by leaders at all levels of society in the phrase, "Not on my watch." Thus, is revealed an extremely important time reference for Christians. If on your 'watch,' you love His appearing, you shall receive a crown from Jesus personally for your pains, even if you die before His Shout! Conversely, if you disregard the imminent aspect during your watch, you risk losing the crown.

Because Jesus' birth, death and resurrection have already transpired, divine protocol as well as natural logic demands we now pursue the study of the imminence of the Rapture, which places us at the next, or Second Watch.

So, as Jesus not only commanded on many occasions that believers watch for His return to earth, He also commanded believers to *watch* for their calling out at the beginning of sorrows in order that "...you may be counted worthy to **escape** all these things that will come to pass..." And in this quote from Luke 21:36, Jesus is referring to *escaping* "...these things that will come to pass..." "...on all those who dwell on the face of the whole earth." (vs. 35) {NKJV}

Note, also, that Jesus alerted listeners that Jacob's Trouble would not eliminate His Return, but rather foreshadow it. Thus, all who miss the Rapture, who repent and turn to Jesus for forgiveness during the Tribulation are encouraged to begin their watch for His return to earth. Every eye, in this case, shall see Him returning, as lightning from the east to the west!

Watching by itself does not automatically impute 'being prepared' for calling out. Watching enables the attention to those postures which aid in making one worthy for the deliverance. Watching, postures and worthiness shall all be examined in their order.

Jesus speaks of His return for His Bride in two aspects, which actually refines the second watch into two separate reflections. One will be for a thief to those unmindful of His promise. That same exact moment will be as in daylight to those eagerly anticipating His calling upward. Paul encourages in I Thess. 5:4, "But you, brethren, are not in darkness, so that this Day should overtake you as a thief." So, believers will not suffer the shock of being accosted as by a thief, though many will be surprised, and some sadly ashamed. {NKJV}

Verse 35, of the previous passage, states, "For as a snare shall it come on all them that dwell on the face of the *whole earth.*" This one sentence contains two phrases that capture the entirety of the Tribulation experience, "...all them ..." and "...whole earth..." "...all them..." would also include both the entire human population and the "...whole earth..." Talk about inclusiveness! Obviously, the only way one can 'escape', (v. 36), catastrophes that are going to encompass the entire population and the whole world is to *get off the planet!* {JB2}

Thus, Jesus is again commanding those who believe His word to prepare to witness these warnings beginning to be fulfilled, that they might be prepared to be taken out worthily, and, as several Apostles agree in later epistles, in order that believers will not be ashamed when He appears.

This appearance is at His elopement with His Bride, as referred to in the subheading of this work, 'A Biblical Chronology of Our Blessed Hope.'

But of course, the 'Day' Paul is referring to in I Thess. 5:2 is that which begins following the Rapture and encompasses the seven-year Tribulation. Then Jesus returns to earth with us, His Bride, to end the Tribulation. The Anti-Christ and Satan's forces are destroyed. Satan is bound and cast into the bottomless pit for a thousand years. {Rev. 20:3, HCSB}

The sheep and goats are separated. The earth is cleansed, and the thousand-year reign ensues.

At the end of the thousand-year reign, Satan is loosed one last time to gather hordes of anti-God earth dwellers for a final assault on Jerusalem. The King of Kings is ready. Satan reaps eternal damnation in the lake of fire with his deceived. This age closes with the Great White Throne Judgment. Then time transitions from the 'Day' to eternity future.

This writing shall scale down the subject matter to the scant reflection of the imminence of the Rapture, that twinkling of an eye described as a theft to some and a divine deliverance for others. The second *distinctly* different phase concerning the prophecies of the Lord's actual return to earth itself is spectacularly micro-scoped in Rev. 1:7 as '...every eye shall see Him.' That's every eye on the planet!

This then leaves us to examine the chronological timeline provided by certain passages throughout the Bible related to the Rapture. We shall see the development of the Blessed Hope doctrine as it threads through Scripture. There are many positions as to the order and time the books of the Old Testament and the New Testament were initially written.

To redeem the time, a suggested outline of Bible book dates and their order of publication are helpful*. This selection will aid in focusing on the development of the Rapture teaching through the ages. To avoid arguments on exact historical placement of proclamations, we shall instead endeavor to gain a perspective on the generally accepted *order in which the prophecies were given. *(pages 227-228)

For this perspective, the dating of each writing, whether Old Testament or New, shall be gathered by comparing dates of accepted Bible timelines. Undoubtedly, such conclusions shall continue to be refined as scholarship advances.

One can readily understand the desire for refining the exact time of publishing each work to more clearly grasp the full measure of intent within each declaration. That time of perfect understanding may elude all scholarship until we *'know even as we are known.'* Hopefully, this continuing work offers some insight into the reality of the Rapture and impending imminent fulfillment. Documented corrections, even post publication of this book, will continually be sought for and received with relish. {I Cor. 13:12, KJV} *{Readers of this Fourth edition: Any remnant books of the earlier editions will provide some understanding of the advancement in study.}*

An excellent prophecy in support of this approach is Mic. 5:2, which foretells the birth of *Ha Maschiach*, the Messiah, seven centuries prior to the event. The specific day is not given in this passage because the reality of the event overshadows the date of the birth itself. Importantly, this prophecy was given in the midst of God's war with Satan.

Acknowledging the ongoing spiritual war helps us to understand God's careful revelations of future events.

So, we endeavor to reaffirm the approach of this coming prophetical event, continuing in confidence of God's Word. Let us acquire a clearer vision of His promise and our deliverance from the coming Tribulation and time of 'Jacob's trouble,' as we grow in the knowledge of the Lord. {Jer. 30:7; & Matt. 24:21}

"Our Blessed Hope," expresses the reality that I, the author of this work, join with all past, present and future believers (even of what scant time is left) who are expecting Jesus at any moment. We do so aware that as Paul emphasized in I Cor. 13:12, '...now I know in part...' And so, we continue to cultivate and refine our anticipation of the Blessed Hope until the shout of the archangel and the trump of God! {KJV}

Paul emphasized this teaching is especially designed that we may be enabled to comfort and strengthen one another. By quelling those natural and most sensible fears concerning the exponential spread of disasters across the world, telegraphing the impending wrath of God soon to fall upon the earth, to which we are not appointed, believers are thus continually refreshed daily for 'occupying' until He Shouts!

We all should be thus duly strengthened and comforted with the uplifting promise that Jesus will shortly be receiving His Bride instantaneously. With this hope then secured firmly within us, we can return to plying the highways, hedges, prisons and pews for all who seek eternal life. Whatever that might entail, forgiveness and/or deliverance, for all in need are eligible for eternal salvation, and the scheduled *'Greatest Ride off Earth!'*

Jesus will 'snatch' His Bride away right on schedule in the twinkling of an eye! And thus, knowing the disciples were encouraged on the restoration of Israel, we may also confidently consider the text and other separate, related prophetical passages assuring of our Blessed Hope.

Meanwhile all disciples through the ages have been empowered by the anointing of the Holy Spirit prophesied by Jesus. Witnesses unto Him are yet going forth from Jerusalem all the way to the uttermost parts of the earth.

In Acts 1:11, two men in white apparel prophesy that Jesus will return. "And while they looked steadfastly toward heaven as he went up, behold, two men stood by them in white apparel: which also said, ye men of Galilee, why stand ye gazing up into heaven? This same Jesus, which is taken up from you into heaven, shall so come in like manner as ye have seen him go into heaven." {KJV}

How had they seen Jesus go? Acts 1:9, "And when he had spoken these things, *while they beheld*, he was taken up; and *a cloud received him* out of their sight." {KJV}

It is fitting the inspired Word reflects the disciples beholding Jesus being taken up. The description dovetails perfectly with Jesus' instruction that believers be *looking up* for His catching away!

As those disciples saw Jesus leave this earth, we who watch shall first hear His Shout and bullet up to meet Him in the sky. Within that same moment all chosen, the dead first, shall be snatched from this planet in the twinkling of an eye! "After that, we who are still alive and are left will be caught up together with them in the clouds to meet the Lord in the air. And so, we will be with the Lord forever." {I Thess. 4:17, NIV}

But no earth dwellers shall see Jesus in the clouds at this point. That sight is reserved for our Lord's return to the earth!

Note by contrast that Rev. 1:7 reveals every eye on earth will see Jesus coming back to the earth itself, "Look, he is coming with the clouds," and "every eye will see him, even those who pierced him"; and "will mourn because of him." So shall it be! Amen." {NIV}

Zechariah 14:4 confirms, "On that day his feet will stand on the Mount of Olives, east of Jerusalem…" {NIV}

But at the Rapture Jesus will also return as a thief to the unprepared. When? At the Shout. In a moment, in the twinkling of an eye. While it is still called 'today.'

Why then had the men rebuked the witnesses to Jesus' ascension for standing around watching the sky? Striving not to land too heavily on this point, the angels were urging the disciples that there wasn't a *moment* to lose!

As Jesus instructed, the time would come when they would see the signs of the end being revealed. It was then they were to obediently begin to 'look up' to watch for His calling out and their escape.

The two had said Jesus would '…come in like manner…' However, Paul states in his description of the event known as the Rapture, speaking of those who are alive and remain that they, "…shall be *caught up* together…in the clouds…" {I Thess. 4:17; KJV}

'*Caught up*' from the KJV Greek '*harpazo*' (say: har-pad'-zo,) rendered by Strong's as: to seize, catch (away, up), pluck, pull, take (by force.)

Quoted from Jerome's Latin Vulgate, 'rapiemur' as documented at the end of this book, and from which we gain the word 'rapture, derived from the root word "*rapio*," speaks of being *violently* snatched up and away.

Further study of this usage softens the interpretation as one discovers the action will be performed out of love created for the 'taken', an atomic moment of Divine ecstasy! The Bride shall be 'swept' away by her Lover! And this event will include first all dead and then all alive in Christ within the same single moment!

Jesus left in the clouds, and he will return in the clouds to receive us! Let us therefore open and examine God's Word to track this glorious path to our elopement with our Groom!

One final note can be recognized here as we close this chapter. An observer to this study, when first asked his view on the Rapture, replied, "...mind your own business..." This was his response to discussing the imminent snatching away of the Church. Continuing, he superiorly intoned "...I believe that *is* in that passage somewhere..."

The referenced verses read, "...that you also aspire to lead a quiet life, to mind your own business, and to work with your own hands, as we commanded you, that you may walk properly toward those who are outside, and that you may lack nothing." {I Thess.4:11-12; NKJV}

Out of context, the phrase 'mind your own business' can easily be interpreted as an admonition to keep the teaching to one's self. But in rightly dividing the word you can be assured Paul was speaking to the walk of a believer towards others, especially believers accepting and anticipating the imminent Rapture.

In verse 10, and in fact from the opening of that chapter, Paul is instructing the Thessalonian congregation on the daily walk for a Christian among others, especially among those who are also in the Lord.

Specifically, in relation to the teaching of the imminent Rapture Paul is about to detail, all those who accept the promise of the Rapture understand more fully its temporal benefits. Knowing Jesus shall catch His Bride away before the wrath of God falls on the earth and its inhabitants encourages a sense of peace. Panic and all other irresponsible conduct can more easily be avoided, cultivating instead a life of peaceful, industrious labor, knowing elopement is coming at any moment.

We know this because the Apostle, having given this direction for a quiet and peaceable life, then details the blockbuster prophecy of the Rapture in the concluding verses 13-18 of this same chapter.

And Paul makes this revelation as he points out in I Thess. 4:13, "...we do not want you to be ignorant." {ISV}

Here Paul juxtaposes the eternal hope of believers against the total lack of hope of those who live and die without Jesus, having no hope in this life or in eternity.

Ergo, our concentration on the second watch in anticipation of the imminent, any moment, snatching away of the Bride of Messiah by Ha Maschiach Himself!

Most notably previewed by Paul and John, the only two Christians, of the few in history to have experienced the Rapture already, that shall at any moment, among those dead in Christ, again be Raptured a second time! (More of this later! The Lord Willing!){I Thess. 4:17}

All of this that we may fulfill Paul's admonition to "... comfort one another with these words."

Chapter Three

Ecstasy Divine

Our Eloping with Jesus

As days continue to plummet headlong into the tomorrows of the future, even so certain Christians have an especially exciting prospect looming that is becoming increasingly hard to ignore, especially for we relatively few who believe in the imminent Rapture. All in Christ shall be raptured. However, not all in Christ shall receive the crown of righteousness. Why? Because they are among those who are not 'loving' His manifestation.' {II Tim. 4:8, Young's Literal Translation}

Jesus promised Peter He would return and receive Peter, and by extension His Bride into prepared mansions that we might for all eternity be with Him. The nut of this work shall be to examine how close we are to this prophecy's launch.

Although no one knows the day or hour of fulfillment, Jesus did warn of end times' trials that would befall the entire earth and population. He also tipped believers on the beginning of these catastrophes across the earth, which shall include exponentially increasing earthquakes in diverse places, wars, floods, rumors of wars and so forth. His warning to watch for these disasters was in order that the observant might escape the coming Tribulation. Do these troubles sound familiar?

Paul informed the Corinthian congregation of this promise, which had been couched in 'mystery' in ages past, "Behold, I shew you a mystery; we shall not all sleep, but we shall all be changed..." {I Cor.: 15:51-52, KJV}

Paul designated this sublime proclamation as 'Our Blessed Hope'. His teachings as well as instances throughout Holy Writ point directly and indirectly to the reality and fulfillment of this powerful prophecy that shall affect, by various inclusions, the entire planet. That means everyone, dead and alive.

Two significant aspects of this doctrine have faded into the mists as the centuries and millennia have rolled out. We shall endeavor to refocus back to these Rapture aspects that have been lost over time.

Firstly, that prophetic call ***to watch for and anticipate*** the shout of Jesus which initiates the event-time for Christians as being encapsulated in the 'twinkling of an eye." Jesus snatches away his Bride from the multiplying catastrophes shrouding over the world. This will be much like being rescued from a battlefield under the beginning attack of a horrendous bombardment.

Recognized as 'the imminence' or any moment calling out, daily anticipation of this razor's edge immediacy strengthens believers for each and every moment leading to the Shout!

As pressures of this present age continue to exponentially increase, Christians are encouraged to not only take one day at a time, the obedient are schooled to navigate each and every moment through each day as it evolves.

And the second forgotten aspect of the doctrine of the Rapture is the recognition that this scripturally described 'violent snatching away' of the Bride shall nonetheless be **_enrapt in God's love._** Believers can be assured the tearing away from the earth shall be a whisking up into the heavens, ever so divinely controlled by God's loving grace.

Yes, the love aspect, has somehow been diminished through the ages, to become in these last days embarrassingly absent from the proclamation of the event.

A brief glance at Paul's marvelous and storied exposition of love's reach in I Cor. 13 comforts even the simplest mind in quest of God's unfailing care. Gifts of humility abound in this Divine offering.

Christendom has wandered so far from these central realities of the event of Our Blessed Hope as to inspire confused teachings that not only deny the prophecy altogether but proclaim in the process that the 'erring' Rapture doctrine proposes 'a psychology of fear and destruction'.

So suggested ordained Lutheran minister Barbara Rossing, a teaching professor of New Testament, at the Lutheran School of Theology, Chicago, in the publication of her book, "The Rapture Exposed," July 5, 2005, per example. Her book dismissed Rapture theology out of hand, with a confused allegorical interpretation of Scripture popular in liberal schools. This author reviewed her work on Amazon, entitling the perspective, "Our Blessed Hope?" *(emphasis on the '?', author's note)*

It is necessary to cultivate His love above all other priorities, while striving to fulfill His leading. Even so, we must challenge *'in love'* faulty theologies at odds with the proclamation of Our Blessed Hope. For we are to '...contend for the faith once delivered to the saints.' And this we shall strive to lovingly do! {Jude 1:3, Darby Bible Translation}

It shall remain, however, the first order of obedience that we may all search out "...whatever is true...noble... just...pure...lovely...and of good report, that if there is any virtue, and if there is anything praiseworthy," we may then "meditate on these things." {Phil. 4:8, NKJV}

There are loads of good books, articles, sermons and expositions, even tons available online, to any who wish to augment their study of this topic from favorable yet also academically sound scholarship. Here is one excellent quote from an examination that provides a brief, but doctrinally sound overview of the Rapture teaching:

[From Porter L. Barrington, "*The Christian Life Master Outlines and Study Notes, Group XI, The Last Days, #49, The Four Phases of the Second Coming, page 60, 49-A— The Rapture of the Church (1 Thessalonians 4:13-18, page 1211); The Christian Life Bible with Old and New Testaments, the New King James Version, Thomas Nelson Publishers, 1985 : — the word 'rapture' (caught up physically, and in* <u>ecstasy</u>*) has come into popular use today to refer to the Lord Jesus' coming for His bride (the church), to lift her up into the heavens (v. 17). It comes from the word 'rapio' in the Latin Bible's translation of this verse. One raptured is 'lifted up' in* <u>love</u>*.*"]

This view will hopefully become apparent throughout this book. Continual reference is made in Scripture to the 'good' of this prophecy, causing those in the first century church to look forward *eagerly* for its fulfillment. That our promised deliverance, as proclaimed by Jesus in the Olivet discourse, from continuously multiplying

31

world-wide disasters spanning seven years, can be so distorted by some interpreters as to be called a 'destructive reading of the Biblical story,' confounds reasoning.

Scholastic weight and measure balances against this grave misconception. A multitude of scriptural references uphold thoughtful consideration of the _loving_, though atomically shocking elopement of His Bride by Jesus!

Can a bride be anything but ecstatic at the anticipation of her groom's promised elopement?

God's eternal wisdom is evident in His leaving out the specific day and hour of fulfillment for the prophecy. God knows exactly how long in human-time the passage of days to the very moment of His calling out the Church. After all, He causes the sun to rise.

And so, we get the initial instruction embedded in Matt. 6:34, to "...take no thought for tomorrow." Paul continues the teaching warning of "...while it is still called today." James and Peter both enjoin that Jesus, the Judge, is "...at the door."

God's timing has always been shaped thusly. Our generation has arrived at Heb. 10:25, discovering, we now, "...see the Day approaching."

In anticipation of His Shout, we grow in wonder knowing that 'the twinkling of an eye,' shall be Divine ecstasy for all we who are alive and remain.

Peter & Paul's Certain Prophecies

Nearly two decades after the first written Apostolic letters referencing the Rapture, Peter gives us one final undergirding for this look into the Bible's confirmation on the reality of the imminent Rapture.

II Peter 1:19 encourages the reader, "We have also a more sure word of prophecy; whereunto ye do well that ye take heed, as unto a light that shineth in a dark place, until the day dawn, and the day star arise in your hearts..." {KJV}

In addition to Peter's affirmation of this '*more sure word of prophecy*,' what made Paul so convinced his own understanding of the Rapture prophecy was accurately proclaimed? Because:

Paul had already experienced the Rapture some several years prior to writing I Thess.! {II Cor. 12:1-4}

Yes! Paul's testifying to his own passed Rapture event comes about in II Cor. as he feels compelled to once again defend his authority and position in Messiah against the naysayers of his day. Establishing his 'street creds' nearly a decade beyond I Thess., in Chapter 10, Paul begins a lengthy disclosure of his service for the Lord, all of this that he might even, in verse 16, "...preach the Gospel in the regions beyond..." {NIV}

It was ever Paul's unction to magnify Jesus and His Gospel to the ends of the earth.

In this passage of several chapters Paul records his confidence in the Lord's leading and provision in his life. Paul was compelled by many attacks on his character and authority to reaffirm his *apostleship* that he might freely proclaim the Gospel of Jesus Christ.

Thus, his enumerating the various blessed opportunities given him leads to the most astounding revelation to that point, as he recalls being raptured to Heaven several years prior to traveling to Thessalonica.

II Cor. 12:2, "I know a man in Christ who fourteen years ago was caught up to the third heaven.

> *Whether it was in the body or out of the body I do not know—God knows." {NIV}*

He does not include as many specific details as he bestows in his Thessalonian letters and elsewhere because he's focusing on the fact that it did happen rather than the description of the event itself! We can deduce that 14 years prior to the writing of II Cor. would have been several years before Paul wrote I & II Thess.; even possibly near the period Paul records in Galatians that he journeyed to Jerusalem to meet with the leading apostles including James, the half-brother of Jesus and author of the Book of James. {Gal. 1:18-19}

Focusing on this utterance the reader discovers a most astounding testimony. God raptured Paul to Heaven! And God raptured Paul to Heaven several years before Paul wrote to the Thessalonicans. The verse includes the phrase 'caught up', identical to I Thess. 4:17. It is the same in the English and Greek. In Jerome's Latin Vulgate, the phrase emanates from the same root word, 'rapio.'

But I Thess. proclaims 'rapiemur', the Latin term speaking of a *future* tense action to be 'violently' snatched up. II Cor. employs the past participle 'raptum' revealing Paul's sense of having been 'plundered' or abducted as a victim or 'prey'. So, Paul is instructing believers to be ready for an event he has already experienced and is therefore totally confident of his encouragement. As a 'plunder' or 'prey' Paul is transported instantaneously to the third Heaven, into paradise. {II Cor. 12:2, LXX}

Paul has already taken the greatest ride off earth! And it has been revealed to him that in this same way all believers in Jesus shall experience the identical event. Early in his ministry, Paul proclaimed to the

Thessalonicans he was expecting to be caught up with all other believers who are alive and remain on the earth.

Nearly a decade later, Paul recalls to the Corinthians he has already experienced this divine event early in his Christian life. As wonderful as that Rapture experience was to Paul, he is allowed to witness even greater realities while in Heaven. In II Cor. 12:4, Paul "...*was snatched, ('raptus' = past tense),* away to Paradise and heard things that cannot be expressed in words, things that no human being has a right even to mention." {International Standard Version}

It is only in the closing days of his life, having finished his course, that the least of the Apostles begins to anticipate not just being raised from the dead, but receiving his crown of righteousness for having loved Jesus' appearing throughout his service to his Lord and Savior.

Yet even as he begins to look forward to receiving that crown, he encourages any that shall follow before the Rapture to continue loving and anticipating Jesus' appearing at any moment while it is still called today! For all who are obedient to Paul's instruction to love His appearing shall also themselves receive the 'Crown of Righteousness' from Jesus Himself!

Was this command to look up vastly important, to be watching in anticipation for our Lord's snatching us believers out of this world?

Paul's first epistle, I Thess., and possibly the first published writing of the New Testament, has been divided into five chapters. The Rapture and its imminent expectation are emphasized by closing every chapter.

More significant is Paul's direct command in 5:27:

> *"I charge you by the Lord that this epistle be read unto all the holy brethren."*

Astoundingly, Paul demands the whole congregation be read this entire epistle! That is how important the teaching of the imminent Rapture was to the Apostle Paul. As we hurtle towards that defining moment in world history in continuing acceleration, recognition of Divine importance will only exponentially increase!

Chapter Four

Beginning at the Beginning

b.c. 4004–Genesis
{The First Gospel Proclamation}

The Coming Messiah
Prophesied from the Garden of Eden

Genesis 3:15 is designated the 'Proto Evangelium', the original or first Gospel proclaimed, per Biblical scholars. It provides the first proclamation of the Gospel, the Good News, and the first prophecy of the coming Messiah. This announcement declares the Messiah destroys Satan.

An extremely important distinction of this prophecy concerning the Messiah destroying Satan is that it parenthetically enfolds scores of major prophecies within its parameters. His birth, death, resurrection and the Rapture are among the multitudes of other prophetical points tucked away in this far-reaching proclamation. Acquiring the understanding of these prophecies protects the student of Scripture from confusion when considering the Messiah's comings and goings, which encompass three primary advents.

Job testified to the Third Coming to earth in Job 19:25, "For I know *that* my redeemer liveth, and *that* he shall stand at the latter *day* upon the earth." {KJV}

Our Lord's First coming to earth is prophesied in the famous Mic. 5:2 passage, proclaiming His birth in Bethlehem. His Second coming is prefaced by Paul's announcement of Jesus snatching His Bride away at the Rapture, I Thess. 4:13-18. Zechariah foretells His Third appearance on earth with His Bride to rescue Israel at the end of the Tribulation:

> *"Then the LORD will go out and fight against those nations as when he fights on a day of battle. On that day his feet shall stand on the Mount of Olives that lies before Jerusalem on the east, and the Mount of Olives shall be split in two from east to west by a very wide valley, so that one half of the Mount shall move northward, and the other half southward." {Zech.14:3-4, ESV}*

Parenthetically, Arnold Fruchtenbaum surmises Jesus returns to Jerusalem following His battle with Satan's armies attacking the Jewish hideout in Petra. A key passage he employs for this conclusion comes from Isaiah:

> *"Who is this coming from Edom, from Bozrah, with his garments stained crimson? Who is this, robed in splendor, striding forward in the greatness of his strength? It is I, proclaiming victory, mighty to save. Why are your garments red, like those of one treading the winepress? I have trodden the winepress alone; from the nations no one was with me. I trampled them in my anger and trod them down*

in my wrath; their blood spattered my garments, and I stained all my clothing." {Is. 63:1-3, NIV} {Read: Footsteps of the Messiah}

John the Revelator introduces Jesus' appearance in the Heavens at His Return to earth:

"And I saw heaven opened, and behold, a white horse, and He who sat on it is called Faithful and True, and in righteousness He judges and wages war." {Rev. 19:11-19, NASB}

This fulfillment leads directly to Israel's restoration to their kingdom, as proclaimed in both the Old and New Testaments.

Per example, before disciplining Adam and Eve for succumbing to Satan's temptation for the forbidden fruit, God first curses the serpent's physical existence for the rest of temporal perpetuity. God then condemns Satan's eternal state by proclaiming the coming of *Ha Maschiach*, the Messiah of Israel and the world. {Genesis 3:15}

Prophecies continue to follow proclaiming the advent of the Messiah throughout the *Tanakh*, the Old Testament. This body of Divinely inspired scripture is authenticated by Jesus many times in His references to things 'written'.

Jeremiah prophesied the New Testament era as an example: *"Behold, the days are coming, says the Lord, when I will make a new covenant with the house of Israel and with the house of Judah – **not according to the covenant** that I made with their fathers in the day that I took them by the hand to lead them out of the land of Egypt, My covenant which they broke, though I was a husband to them, says the Lord. **But this is the covenant** that I* *will make with the house of Israel after those days, says the Lord: I will put my law in their minds, and write it on their hearts; and I will be their God, and they shall be my people." {Jer. 31:31-33, NKJV}*

Notice that God does not say that His law will be done away with, but rather that He will 'put my law in their minds, and write it on their hearts...' In the Sermon on the Mount, Jesus underscores God's changeless law saying, *"Do not think that I came to destroy the Law or the Prophets. I did not come to destroy but to fulfill. For assuredly, I say to you, till heaven and earth pass away, one jot or one tittle will by no means pass from the law till all is fulfilled."* {Matt. 5:17-18, NKJV}

In roughly 1490 B.C., just over 1500 years after Enoch was translated, "Then the Lord spoke to Moses, saying: 'Speak to the children of Israel, saying: In the seventh month, on the first day of the month, you shall have a Sabbath-rest, a memorial of blowing of trumpets, a holy convocation.'" {Leviticus 23:23-24, NKJV}

This is the feast of Yom Teruah, the blowing of the trumpets. It was for centuries an obscure feast, which seemed to have no specific or significant meaning.

Following the invoking of the Roman Diaspora in 70 a.d., during the Talmudic period extending to 500 a.d., the name of this feast was changed to Rosh Hashanah, or Head of the Year. This tradition has been suggested as being applied from the earlier dispersion of the children of Israel to Babylon, where during their captivity they grew accustomed to celebrating the Babylonian New Year during this season in which Yom Teruah fell.

However, it is also recognized that Jesus was crucified in the first month of the Jewish Calendar, which would have been Israel's time to celebrate the beginning of the year. Creating this new feast to replace an obscure feast half-way round the calendar would certainly shift any undesirable attention or reminders of the conflicts that arose between the growing number of followers of the Galilean carpenter and the Sanhedrin. The concern becomes manifest when one considers the changing of a feast day instituted by God Himself.

And, of course, Rosh Hashanah has continued to be celebrated with the blowing of the shofar, until this present hour. Evidently, some things never change.

Later in this same period of 1490 B.C. in Num. 10:1-3, the Lord commands Moses to make two special trumpets of silver for a specific purpose, "...you shall use them for calling the congregation and for directing the *'journeying'** of the camps." God then instructs, "When they blow both of them, all the congregation shall gather before you at the door of the tabernacle of meeting." *{NKJV, movement – KJV, journeying}

Also note, the gathering is unto the 'door of the tabernacle'. "[7] Then said Jesus unto them again, Verily, verily, I say unto you, I am the door of the sheep." {John 10:7} And, again, in Numbers 10, verse 7, "[7] But when the congregation is to be gathered together, ye shall blow, but ye shall not sound an alarm."

These trumpets were purposed to call the congregation together and direct their movement. Consider Paul's prophecies in this context. And remember the instruction for the 1st blowing of the trumpet, 'to gather,' and then the second, or final trumpet's warning defined in Strong's Exhaustive Concordance in the Hebrew: 8643. *Te ruw ah' (ter-oo-aw'), from 7321; clamor, i.e. acclamation of joy or a battle-cry; espec. Clangor of trumpets, as an alarm: —alarm, blow (-ing) (of, the) (trumpets), joy, jubilee, loud noise, rejoicing, shout (-ing), (high, joyful) sound (-ing).*

I Thess. 4:16, "For the Lord Himself will descend from heaven with a shout, with the voice of the archangel, and *with the trumpet* of God. And the dead in Christ will rise first." And then, I Cor. 15:52, "...in a flash, in the twinkling of an eye, at the last trumpet." {NASB, NIV}

The Jewish believers would have known exactly the illustration the Ruach Ha Kodesh, the Holy Spirit, was inspiring through the Apostle Paul, using not only the trumpet, but designating the movement on the last blast. During the 40 years of wilderness wandering the children of Israel grew accustomed to responding immediately to the trumpet blast.

Yet, there is an extremely important distinction given by Paul. For he is declaring that when this trumpet command will be blown in the twinkling of an eye, there won't be time to be gathering together physically, as was done in the day of Moses. Inside that twinkle, the moment of translation will be for all concerned, including those leaving and the far greater masses left behind, atomically abrupt! Clearly a *Blast Off*!

In fact, many in the Body who are anticipating His Shout even believe Yom Teruah not merely mirrors the Rapture, but in fact is the adumbration, or foreshadowing of our Blessed Hope. Consider a celebratory offering my wife, Karen, wrote for our Facebook page, *Israel's Light*, heralding this Feast:

HAPPY YOM TERUAH!

In the Torah, the 1st day of the seventh month is to be celebrated as Yom Teruah or The Feast of

Trumpets (Lev. 23:24, Num. 29:1). Teruah means 'shouting' or 'raising a noise'. Make a joyful noise unto the LORD (Psalm 81:1-4). Yom Teruah is a unique holiday because 1) it's the only holiday that begins with a new moon and 2) there is no explicit reason given in the Torah for its observance other than to 'rest' and offer a sacrifice (Num. 29:1, Lev 23:24). After the 2nd Temple was destroyed in 70 A.D., however, the sages of the Mishnah redefined Judaism and associated Yom Teruah with the start of the Jewish civil year. Yom Teruah became known as "Rosh Hashanah" (the head of the year). So, as you celebrate this year meditate on the Feast of Trumpets, consider what the Feast truly represents–shout or raise a noise! If you are a believer in Jesus this should remind you of an imminent event on the horizon recorded in 1 Thessalonians 4:16-18, "For the Lord Himself will descend from heaven with a shout, with the voice of an archangel, and with the trumpet of God. And the dead in Messiah will rise first. Then we who are alive and remain shall be caught up together with them in the clouds to meet the Lord in the air. And thus, we shall always be with the Lord. Therefore comfort one another with these words." When will this happen? No one knows– it is imminent–any moment. Are you ready? Are you listening? What a FEAST that will be–when we are with the LORD. Be comforted with these words. Shalom. {HCSB}

Captivatingly, she wrote this for the Feast of 09-25-2014! My how time does fly! One is reminded in the instruction to rest in Hebrews 4:11, " [11] Let us labour therefore to enter into that rest, lest any man fall after the same example of unbelief." {Au-KJV)

Lest drawing together these similar passages suggests a coincidental relation, let us briefly examine some more Old Testament prophecies. Other passages sketch similar outlines that suggest the mystery of the Bride being 'caught away', but careful examination discloses different revelations.

Nearly nine centuries following God's instructions on the use of the silver trumpets, in 626 B.C., the Prophet Zephaniah is moved to pronounce an amazing promise of deliverance by God in the midst of foretelling forthcoming judgment:

> *"Gather yourselves together, yes, gather together, O undesirable nation, before the decree is issued, or the day passes like chaff, before the Lord's fierce anger comes upon you, before the day of the Lord's anger comes upon you! Seek the Lord, all you meek of the earth, who have upheld His justice, seek righteousness, (and) seek humility. It may be that you will be hidden in the day of the Lord's anger." {Zeph. 2:1-3, NKJV}*

Zephaniah calls those who are heeding God's word to gather together. Proclaimed twice, the repetition to gather is immediately reminiscent of the two blasts from the silver trumpets of the Children of Israel.

Some suggest this prophecy adumbrates the Rapture, missing important distinctions that need clarification.

The prophet continues, warning of the coming judgment of the day of the Lord which shall be delivered in His anger. Urging believers to seek the Lord in meekness, righteousness and humility, the prophet closes the warning with a prophetic hint of promise: "...It may be that you will be hidden in the day of the Lord's anger." Such a slight reference could be easily overlooked by even the most careful scholars.

Here the Zephaniah passage must be carefully connected with God's hiding the Children of Israel during the Tribulation. Two keys are prominent. The first is the action takes place during the day of the Lord's anger, countered against His Thessalonian promise that believers are not appointed to wrath and shall escape. Also, key is the word 'hidden.' This dramatically contradicts the Rapture promise of 'escape' described in Paul's Thessalonian prophecy of believers' dead and alive being 'caught up' as they are, not 'hidden'. {Rev 12:6}

A similarly intriguing passage describing God's watch care of His children, Israel, given in Is. 26:20-21, nearly a century before Zephaniah. "Come, my people, enter thou into thy chambers, and shut thy doors about thee: hide thyself as it were for a little moment, until the indignation be over past." {KJV}

Here the people enter into chambers and shut the doors to hide for a little moment. Also, the reader observes 'the indignation be over past,' not 'escaped' from.

Again, the reader recalls Isaiah prophesying God will hide Israel during the worldwide subjection of God's wrath, namely 'Jacob's trouble,' prophesied in Jeremiah 30:7.

Yet, both Zephaniah's and Isaiah's prophecies synchronize with the very words of Jesus in Luke as He answers the disciples' queries concerning the end of days. They had asked specifically concerning '...what sign will there be when these things are about to take place?" {Luke 21:7, NKJV}

Jesus then expounds on the trials that would befall the earth in the last days. He encourages the disciples not to be 'terrified', an especially interesting turn of phrase considering the escalation of 'terrorist' activities across the planet today. Confirming these O.T. prophecies also afforded Jesus the opportunity to give special hope to His followers:

"Watch ye therefore, and pray always, that ye may be accounted <u>worthy to escape</u> all these things that shall come to pass, and to stand before the Son of man." {Luke 21:36, KJV}

"Hidden in the day of the Lord's anger," is set against, '*that ye may be accounted worthy to escape* all these things that shall come to pass, and to stand before the Son of man." These three prophecies, separated over seven centuries, outline two separate deliverances in the end time's scenario. Isaiah and Zephaniah both speak of being 'hidden' until the wrath is 'over past.' Jesus prophesies an 'escape.'

So, the 'catching away' of Enoch is recorded in approximately 3017 b.c. The establishing of Yom Teruah, the feast of Trumpets takes place approximately 1527 years later in Leviticus in 1490 b.c. Zephaniah, in proclaiming the day of the Lord's anger, outlines the Tribulation nine centuries following the founding of the Feast of Trumpets. Seven centuries on from that point, Jesus divulges to his followers there is a way of escape available as He unfolds the end-of-times trials.

He emphasizes signs of wars and rumors of wars, earthquakes, storms on land and sea, famines, and pestilences. He warns in Matt. 24:8, "All these are but the opening of the birth pains." {ESV}

These catastrophes are at the beginning of the day of the Lord's anger. God delivered Enoch before the flood. He prepared His Chosen people to follow His leading by listening for His trumpet. God instructed His prophet to inform the people they could, by preparing in righteousness, be hidden in the day of the Lord's anger. Yet Jesus, in describing the end of this age, cautioned those with ears to hear that they should watch and pray that they might be worthy to *escape* all that would begin to come on the world.

Trials never arrive in a convenient season. There is never enough time to respond when one is caught in turmoil. Human warning systems are continually being developed and refined, especially as technology advances. But the imbalances of one catastrophe imploding upon another continue to exponentially collide as time escalates without hesitation.

Preparation accepted, no one is ready for unannounced disaster. Tragedy always comes too soon. Yet God has demonstrated by action, preparation and His Word, that His provision always arrives soon enough.

Submission of these passages is by no means intended as an exhaustive list in the Tanakh or New Testament relevant to the Rapture or the Lord's second coming to earth. Again, the hope of the author in providing this study is to aide believers and seekers of truth steppingstones through Scripture from Genesis to Revelation that enforce at least a consideration of the Rapture, Our Blessed Hope. And from that consideration a path to comfort and strengthening for the day. Hopefully even a crown or two?

So, before we venture beyond the four centuries of silence that follow the closing of Malachi's days, let us return to the opening of the Tanakh, the Old Testament. Here we can begin our study of the observable, multiplying prophecies that direct those who will believe to the purifying anticipation of our Blessed Hope.

Chapter Five

Old Testament Rapture & Return Reflections

b.c. 3017—Genesis Rapture
b.c. 1491-1000—Psalms
b.c. 971-560—II Kings
b.c. 487—Zechariah
b.c. 485—Nehemiah
b.c. 397—Malachi

Genesis

Holy Writ first introduces the reader to the concept of the Rapture, perhaps surprisingly to many, in Genesis, the first book of the Torah.

We mentioned in the last chapter that God delivered Enoch before the flood deluged the earth. Let's take a closer look at the life of Enoch.

Chapter Five, verse 24 declares: "And Enoch walked with God, and he was not, for God took him." {ESV}

Astoundingly, "...Enoch walked with God; *and he was not, for God took him.*"

To the student of the Bible this passage can create great confusion. First of all, the son of Jared was actually the 'second' Enoch of Biblical documentation recorded to be born on the earth! One is thus obligated to differentiate between the first and the second Enoch, in the same way that the student of Scripture must delineate between the first and second Adam, rightly dividing the word of truth.

In Chapter Four of Genesis, after Cain slew Abel, he traveled to the land of Nod. And there he fathered his firstborn son, Enoch. Little of personal life is noted of this first Enoch, whose name from the Hebrew means 'initiated or dedicated.' Cain did build a city called after his son, Enoch. The rest of Cain's descendants contribute scant additional historical notes.

Jubal was the father of musicians. Tubal-Cain the father of metal craftsmen. The first Lamech sadly became a murderer like his father. A mere listing of other descendants marks the family verses of Gen. 4. Curiously, many of Cain's descendants are given the same names or similar to those of Seth's progeny.

Here is an early example of Paul's instruction to Timothy concerning rightly dividing the word. "Study to shew thyself approved unto God, a workman that needeth not to be ashamed, rightly dividing the word of truth." {*II Tim. 2:15, KJV*}

It also must be acknowledged that often frustration is rightly voiced concerning Biblical genealogies. Questions are raised as to importance, relevance, and purpose concerning these records of lineage. Without the support of answers to these important questions the repetition of family genealogies can be viewed as tiresome, and superfluous. So, in this use of the same or similar names bestowed upon two different lines of descendants of Adam, trailing off into two different lines of descent, the application of rightly dividing the word of truth provides the answer to the intent of their inclusions.

Again, a quick, short review of this genealogy affirms that little is made of Cain's offspring. But eternal blessing springs from the line of Seth, Gen. 5:1-3. Firstly, God actually reforges the opening narrative of the beginning of mankind:

> *"This is the book of the generations of Adam. In the day that God created man, in the likeness of God made he him; male and female created He them; and blessed them and called their name Adam, in the day when they were created. And Adam lived an hundred and thirty years, and begat a son in his own likeness, after his image; and called his name Seth."* {KJV}

So begins the line that leads to the, only momentarily, more obscure second Enoch. By the writing of I Chronicles, 1:3, some 2500 years later, the second Enoch would even be heralded in the line of the Patriarchs. This is confirmed by the preceding appearance of his father Seth in that genealogy.

It must first be observed that God's inspiring the proclamation that His creation was '*blessed*' also sets apart the second line of Enoch. "Blessed" signifies 'happy and approved of God.'

Additional support is made apparent by the continual blessing of God in Seth's line, exemplified by Enoch, Methuselah and Noah.

Marginalizing Cain's line in 5:3, God remolds the progression of His creation with: *"And Adam lived an hundred and thirty years, and begat a son in his own likeness, after his image; and called his name Seth:"* And it is from this line of progenitors that Enoch number two is born. {KJV}

From thus is developed the captivating moment in Gen. 5:24, where this same man called Enoch is walking with God and suddenly vanishes without a trace.

In that passage the verse simply states, "And he (Enoch) was not, for God took him." There is no additional comment. One moment the man is walking with God and the next moment he is gone.

Three millennia later, in Luke 3:37, the second Enoch is recorded in the genealogy of Jesus. Yet, even counting this New Testament verification, few personal details are recorded about this second Enoch, either in the Tanakh or the New Testament, establishing only that he was a Godly man.

Gen. 5:1 opens by listing the genealogy or family tree that begins with Adam. In that listing Jared was the sixth-generation patriarch from Adam, and the father of the second Enoch, who was pronounced in the Book of Jude, Adam's seventh son. Adam lived 930 years. His son, Seth, lived 912 years. Seth's son, Enosh, lived 905 years. Enosh had a son, Cainan, who lived 910 years. Cainan's son, Mahalalel, lived 895 years. Mahalalel's son, Jared, lived 962 years.

Jared's son, Enoch, lived 365 years and then was translated. Over three millennia later, God hints at His dealing with Enoch through Is. 57:1, "The righteous man perishes, and no one lays it to heart; devout men are taken away, while no one understands. For the righteous man is taken away from calamity…" {ESV}

Enoch was the father of Methuselah. Enoch's prescient, (showing knowledge of events before they take place), naming of Methuselah was revealed in the defining of his name: 'when he dies, judgment.' Methuselah lived 969 years, making him the longest-lived human recorded in world history. A week following his death the flood came.

All of the men preceding the second Enoch, and then his son Methuselah, lived nearly 895 years or longer before they died. And each of them, including Enoch, had other sons and daughters besides the children named, though genealogy was established by recording the names of the first-born sons.

But Enoch, who was born at the time Adam was 622 years old, had lived only 365 years when God took him. And Enoch vanished a mere 18 years following Adam's death. Death to the first created man must have been a shock to many, though not a total surprise. But Enoch's departure was not only out of the norm but premature, compared to Adam's longevity. Most of Adam's descendants were still alive when Enoch was taken by God.

Enoch knew, and more importantly was known personally by all of the Patriarchs up to Methuselah. There was substantial testimony from all these of the earliest events of creation to the Flood. Included would have been the witness of Enoch's Rapture.

Enoch's short life was over 5 centuries less than the norm for each of all his predecessors or his son, Methuselah, who lived the longest at 969.

In other words, Adam's son, Seth, was 492 when Enoch was born. This shortfall additionally shows Enoch was a man taken away before his natural life-cycle had been completed. He was not a man born out of time but rather a man *taken out of* his time.

More astoundingly, all of Adam's descendants, from Seth through Lamech were alive at the time of Enoch's translation. That would include Seth, Enosh, Cainan, Mahalalel, Jared, Methuselah, and his firstborn, Lamech. Each of these men were witness not only to the life of Adam but to the time of the disappearance of Enoch, if not in fact actual eye-witnesses to the event itself.

Another confirming factor of Enoch's translation is Noah's birth. For Noah knew seven of the descendants in Adam's line, namely Seth, Enosh, Cainan, Mahalalel, Jared, Lamech and Methuselah. Noah would have been 14 years old when Seth died in 2962 b.c. They would have shared with Noah individually, and corporately at family gatherings. That would have had to include Adam's creation and life as well as Enoch's birth, and rapture. Noah would have had at least second-hand knowledge of Enoch's miraculous translation at the age of 365.

Enoch's departure was so significant to Hebrew history that in the New Testament, Jude, the brother of James, author of the Book of James, who was also, like James, the half-brother of Jesus (Matt. 13:55), reveres Enoch as a prophet. Jude quotes Enoch as prophesying about the end times, "Behold, the Lord comes with ten thousands of His saints, to execute judgment on all..." {Jude 1:14-15, NKJV}

From this prophecy the reader is reminded God had already set specific, eternal judgment for the end of time, and that He will be bringing with Him back to earth a host of His saints. As Jesus prepares to return with His Bride at the end of the Tribulation to deliver Israel, John notes, "...His wife hath made herself ready." {Rev. 19:7, KJV}

And Jude thereby not only corroborates the Genesis account of Enoch's genealogical pedigree but includes a prophetic word concerning the Return of Jesus to the earth "...to execute judgment on all..."

One additional note must be retrieved from this genealogical pool of information. Lamech was the father of Noah. Without regressing into all of the math available in Genesis chapters Five through Seven, it is yet noteworthy that Lamech was 682 years of age when God commanded Noah to begin to build the Ark.

Lamech lived another 95 years, dying at the age of 777, just five years before the onslaught of the worldwide flood, which shall be mentioned historically by Jesus nearly two-and-a-half millennia hence. And Jesus' reference shall focus not merely on the end of the age but include another reminder of the imminent Rapture. (More on this in Chapter Six.)

> *Imperatively, let the record show that fossil evidence of a global flood continues to be available across the planet for those drawn to the debate over a world-wide flood versus a localized downpour. Contact Tom DeRosa, www.creationstudies. org; or Ken Ham, www.answersingenesis.org to initiate an in-depth scientifically scholastic study of the Bible's support of the global flood.*

Lamech's father, Methuselah, lived an additional five years and went to be with his Lord a week before the flood came upon the earth.

Lamech and Methuselah were the last two patriarchs alive from the line of Adam that witnessed Enoch's disappearance, and then witnessed Noah's century of preaching judgment to come upon the earth while he was building the ark. One cannot but be reminded of the Biblical injunction that all claims be established at the testimony of two witnesses. {Deuteronomy 17:6}

Certain Rabbinical scholars consider the Tanakh the sole Word of God, discounting the New Testament. If that were true, the only word from God that would exist about either of the first two Enochs would be the testimony given in Genesis.

If there had been no further word concerning the second Enoch, the question would necessarily be begged as to why even mention this Enoch in the narration in the first place. Enoch's brief inclusion and mysterious disappearance in the narrative would have been beyond superfluous. More than being unnecessary it would have been glaringly pointless. In other words, it would have been apobetically without purpose.

We must then forward to Rom. 15:4 for direction. "For whatever things were written before {speaking of the Tanakh and the Prophets} were written for our learning, that we through the patience and comfort of the scriptures might have hope." {KJV}

Thus, we understand for starters that the vanishing 'Enoch' passage is written for our hope. It then cannot be coincidental that the passage mirrors our Blessed Hope, the Rapture.

But many passages and verses throughout the Holy Bible are made available for our hope, as Rom. 15:4 immediately declares. So, we must delve deeper into the purpose of God's reason for Enoch's biographical notation to better understand connecting his disappearance to the Rapture event.

In the New Testament/Brit Chadashah Heroes of Faith, Chapter 11, Enoch's vanishing is explained with more depth. "By faith Enoch was taken away so that he did not see death, and was not found, because God had taken him; for before he was taken, he had this testimony, that he pleased God. But without faith it is impossible to please Him, for he who comes to God must believe that He is, and that He is a rewarder of those who diligently seek Him." {Heb. 11:5-6, NKJV}

This verse reveals the key ingredient for a Christian life: faith. Faith is the priming element in receiving the teaching and understanding of all scripture, including the Rapture and its imminence. 'Without *faith* it is impossible to please Him.' There is, again, no mere coincidence in the application of faith to describe Enoch's vanishing and Paul's prophecy that the Bride of Messiah will be taken imminently, without hesitation.

Here then is first described the miracle Jesus also prophesied to Martha in John 11:26 – "And whosoever liveth and believeth in me shall never die. Believest thou this?" "…shall never die" mirrors Enoch's disappearance while simultaneously pointing to the future snatching away of the Bride of Messiah. {KJV}

Thus, it is easily seen that Enoch was taken by God alive, that he might not see death, even before he had reached his prime of life. Remember the average age in Enoch's day was roughly 900 years, and he was taken at the early age of 365. He walked with God; he pleased God, because he believed in God and diligently sought the company of God.

Again, the foreshadowing of the Rapture is documented in the encouragement to all future believers as bestowed through the life of Enoch. His life is an example of God's special blessing of rewards to those who diligently seek Him. Thus are believers encouraged by Enoch's faith that they should walk with God.

Note Heb. 11:5 begins, "By faith Enoch was taken away so that he did not see death." Enoch believed God and so was taken away before the deluge of the flood that was coming upon the whole earth. {NKJV}

What clearer picture of the imminent Rapture is necessary? Enoch walked, not ran, with God. He waited upon Him. One cannot ignore here Proverbs 27:18, "Whoso keepeth the fig tree shall eat the fruit thereof: so he that waiteth on his master shall be honoured." {KJV}

The world was sinking deeper and deeper into sin. But Enoch continued with God. Enoch believed God and was suddenly and abruptly taken up to be with God. He vanished, without a trace.

Those who are observant understand that Enoch was taken, as Hebrews explains, because he '...pleased God.' He had faith in God. And having that faith pleased God, who without faith cannot be pleased.

In fact, the Word informs the reader that "...without faith it is impossible to please God, for whoever comes to him must believe that he exists and that he rewards those who diligently search for him. {Heb. 11:6, ISV}

Without question Enoch diligently sought the company of God to the point of walking with Him right up into heaven!

So, we see that Enoch put his faith into action, not only talking the talk but walking the walk! And Enoch believed that putting action to his faith would gain him God's pleasure and thus God's reward.

This is a reflection of Heb. 11: 1, "Now, faith is the substance of things hoped for, the evidence of things not seen." {KJV}

When Jesus told Martha, "...And whoever lives and believes in Me shall never die..." he was making this statement having just proclaimed, "...he who believes in Me, though he may die, he shall live..." {John 11:25-26, NKJV}

So, which is it? Does a person die and then meet Jesus? Or, does a person who lives meet Jesus and then never die? Both are actually right.

Paul explains in I Thess. 4:16-17 that the dead in Christ shall rise first and then 'we' who are alive and remain shall be caught up *with* them, ever to be with the Lord. This statement is made in the present tense. Paul was speaking in the present tense and so at that point of writing he was including himself in the catching away. The Word proclaims itself to be God-breathed, given by inspiration of God, II Tim. 3:16, and therefore infallible.

But Paul was put to death some years later. So, was Paul speaking prematurely and therefore in error? Even though Paul said, 'we who are alive and remain', nevertheless Paul died. He had his head chopped off outside of Rome some seventeen years after writing I Thess. 4:17, "After that, we who are still alive and are left will be caught up together with them in the clouds to meet the Lord in the air. And so, we will be with the Lord forever." {NIV}

But, praise the Lord, Paul wrote to Timothy one last time as he awaited execution at the chopping block.

This epistle was written in the spring of 68 a.d., approximately four years following his first letter to

59

Timothy. About 17 years had elapsed between Paul writing I Thess. and II Tim.

We can peek over Paul's shoulder as he writes in II Tim. 4:6-8 and following:

"For I am already being poured out as a drink offering, and the time of my departure is at hand. I have fought the good fight, I have finished the race, I have kept the faith. Finally, there is laid up for me the crown of righteousness, which the Lord, the righteous Judge, will give to me on that Day, and not to me only but also to all who have loved His appearing." {NKJV}

The man that had prophesied first to the Thessalonicans that "...the dead in Christ shall rise first: Then we which are alive and remain shall be caught up together with them in the clouds to meet the Lord in the air," was now being led by the Holy Spirit in updating the details of the prophecy from a personal perspective. A decade later, four years before his execution, he is still reaffirming his continuing position in Phil. 3:14, 'I press toward the goal for the prize of the *upward call* of God in Christ Jesus.' {I Thess. 4:16-17, KJV; NKJV}

But now, writing II Timothy, he himself is no longer listening for the 'upward call' of God's trumpet! He has finished his course and he is ready to depart to ever be with the Lord. Inadvertently, Paul is acknowledging that he is being promoted to the ranks of the 'dead in Christ' that shall rise first, though he himself, soon to be absent from the body, shall immediately be present with the Lord!

Prophetically, even Paul's execution silhouettes the imminence of the Rapture. He writes Timothy, "…the time of my departure is at hand…" {II Tim. 4:6, KJV}

Paul does not give Timothy the day and time of the beheading, only that the beheading is 'at hand' and going to be carried out soon in Paul's present reality. Declaring his departure to be 'at hand,' hearkens immediately to both Peter and James' individual proclamations of Jesus being 'at the door.'

Although Paul had assured the Corinthians a handful of years before that, "For we know in part and we prophesy in part," now Paul was certain of his execution. He did not know the day or hour, but he knew his time was at hand! {I Cor. 13:9, NIV}

The Lord prophesied in Damascus to Ananias, in Acts 9:16 that He would reveal to Paul "…what great things he must suffer for my name's sake." Paul was now humbling himself to be "…poured out as a drink offering…" {King James 2000; Phil. 2:17, ESV}

And now, following the Philippian jail epistle to Timothy, his beloved disciple and son in the faith, as Paul prepares for execution, he avows the reward that awaits him.

And not Paul only, but '…all those who *have loved* His appearing…' Paul is prophesying the bestowing of a crown of reward for the action of all those who have anticipated the calling out at the Rapture. He posits the anticipation in the future, looking back from heaven to those, '…who have loved…' His appearing. So, here before us we have the written words of the most prominently documented Apostle on record prophesying, reaffirming and submitting with his near death-bed testimony his bedrock belief in the reality of the imminent Rapture, as he has been preaching and teaching from early in his ministry.

Paul was merely proclaiming what the Holy Spirit revealed to him and empowered him to preach and teach to all believers. This Blessed Hope, the miracle translation first enacted nearly 4,000 years before in the person of Enoch, was the prophecy revealed in personal detail to Paul.

Job 7:6 proclaims, "My days are swifter than a weaver's shuttle…" Certainly, Paul was aware of this truth as he now prepared to cross the finish line. He was content, preparing to meet his Lord and Savior again, this time under far better circumstances than when they had first met on the road to Damascus. Paul had been looking forward to this meeting his entire Christian life and had even joyfully admitted in Phil. 1:23, that he had a "…desire to depart, and to be with Christ; which is far better…" For Paul it would be none too soon. However, he knew also that it would be exactly in God's time. {KJV}

Psalms

For brevity's sake we again emphasize here that we shall not try to forge a complete survey of O.T. passages connected with the imminent Rapture. Nor shall we list all of the references to His earthly return.

Paul reveals in I Cor. 15:51 that the imminent Rapture doctrine is in fact a mystery that he is at that point opening to the Corinthian congregation. It behooves the student of scripture to recognize God's imparting to Tanakh prophets His intentions. "Indeed, the Sovereign LORD never does anything until he reveals his plans to his servants the prophets." {Amos 3:7, NLT}

This would include His Return to the Earth as prophesied by Job. "For I know *that* my redeemer liveth, and *that* he shall stand at the latter *day* upon the earth..." {Job 19:25, KJV}

Psalms is another excellent focal point for such confirmation. Passages such as Psalm 96:13, "Let all creation rejoice before the LORD, for he comes, he comes to judge the earth. He will judge the world in righteousness and the peoples in his faithfulness." Also 98:9, "... let them sing before the LORD, for he comes to judge the earth. He will judge the world in righteousness and the peoples with equity." These, only per example, are excellent reminders of the times God inspired the prophets to declare that He reveals the end from the beginning. {NIV}

Yet, our focus must continually return to the imminent ... a speck of time hidden within a mystery of God's devising, the imminent Shout of Jesus for His Bride. And here, Psalms does not disappoint.

In Psalm 47:47:1-7, Au-KJV,
(We glean a hidden gem amongst the fold.)

[1] "O clap your hands, all ye people;
shout unto God with the voice of triumph.
[2] For the LORD most high *is* terrible;
he is a great King over all the earth.
[3] He shall subdue the people under us,
and the nations under our feet.
[4] He shall choose our inheritance for us,
the excellency of Jacob whom he loved. Selah.
[5] God is gone up with a shout,
the LORD with the sound of a trumpet.

⁶ Sing praises to God, sing praises:
sing praises unto our King, sing praises.
⁷ For God *is* the King of all the earth:
sing ye praises with understanding."

Note the opening of ecstatic joy! Jesus is introduced. His pre-eminence is declared. His eternal plan unfolds, the lightening Shout revealed, the Rapture an event already transacted! "... God is gone up ...", the sound of a trumpet echoing in his wake ... Even through His word, the Lord establishes the Rapture happens before it can even be imagined, His exit with His Bride having already taken place, the action itself accompanying the Shout!

Moreover, the Lord polishes His prophetic revelation of our inheritance in consistence centuries later through I Peter 1: 4, Au-KJV,

"To an inheritance incorruptible, and undefiled, and that fadeth not away, reserved in heaven for you,"

Again, our Lord displays the perfection of His word ...

"Every word of God *is* pure:" {Prov. 30:5a, Au-AKJV}

Thus, God's word cannot but hint at this glorious moment, likening Jesus' appearance for His Bride as the appearance of the morning summer sun:

"Which is as a bridegroom coming out of his chamber, and rejoiceth as a strong man to run a race." {Psalm 19:5, Au-KJV}

II Kings

Another O.T. passage clearly points to the upward call of the Rapture. II Kings 2:1-11 records how the Lord would 'take' the prophet Elijah to heaven in a whirlwind on a chariot of fire. Witnessed by his anointed replacement, Elisha, Elijah was 'taken' to Heaven following his final three assignments. He anointed a king of Syria and a king of Israel. Then he chose Elisha as his replacement for prophet.

These prophetical acts were God's final commands to Elijah, after he had fled into the wilderness from Queen Jezebel, who had vowed to kill him. The span of time between Elisha's anointing and Elijah's departure was 10 years.

Interestingly, as Elijah approached his point of embarkation, he asked Elisha, "Ask what I shall do for thee, before I be *taken* away from thee." Strong's Concordance suggests a wide swath of definitive variations possible from the Hebrew for 'take' and 'taken.' {II Kings 2:9, KJV}

Scholastic review narrows the Hebrew to meaning simply 'taken.' Causing the incident to yet garner additional interest for once more mirroring the future snatching of the Bride.

Others may include, Psalm 47:6-7,
"Sing praises to God, sing praises:
sing praises unto our King, sing praises.
For God is the King of all the earth:
sing ye praises with understanding."

and Ps. 95:7-9,

"For he is our God;
and we are the people of his pasture,
and the sheep of his hand.
Today if ye will hear his voice,
8 harden not your heart, as in the provocation,
and as in the day of temptation in the wilderness:
9 when your fathers tempted me,
proved me, and saw my work."

15 *while it is said, To day if ye will hear his voice,*
harden not your hearts, as in the provocation." {& Heb.
3:15; Au-KJV}

Zechariah

In a.d. 487 God moves the prophet Zechariah to speak
of the Lord's return to earth. It is noteworthy that this
prophecy of the end times should be given just prior to
the end of Old Testament revelations. Four score years
from this prophecy God would become silent for four
hundred years until the birth of Messiah.

"Behold, the day of the Lord is coming...I will
gather all the nations to battle against Jerusalem;
the city shall be taken, the houses rifled, and the
women ravished. Half of the city shall go into
captivity, but the remnant of the people shall
not be cut off from the city. Then the Lord will
go forth and fight against those nations...And
in that day His feet will stand on the Mount of
Olives, which faces Jerusalem on the east. And
the Mount of Olives shall be split in two...Thus

the Lord my God will come, and all the saints with You." {Zech. 14:1-5, NKJV excerpts.}

Lifting the veil into the future, Zechariah continues to build on the revelations given of the Lord's return. For more details of the day of the Lord the reader is encouraged to read Zechariah in its entirety.

For our purposes, note the day of the Lord begins on earth with Tribulation battles being described at the end of the seven years. Within the prophecy, the Lord brings with Him '...all the saints..." The Rapture having already taken place, His saints are therefore already with Him.

Nehemiah

A most astounding entry may be discovered in Nehemiah 8:1-12 of the Authorized King James Version. Ezra is told to "... bring the Book of the Law of Moses, which the Lord had commanded Israel." Ezra did so and read from it. Careful consideration reveals for the reader the day was most propitious. "... on the first day of the seventh month."

The book of the Law was of course the Tanakh, the Old Testament, and the portion to read would be that which was dedicated to the feast day being celebrated. Which in this instance was 'Yom Teruah/Day of Shouting' for war, alarm or joy, depending. Also known as 'The Feast of Trumpets', which has been changed on the Jewish calendar to 'Rosh Ha Shanah/Head of the Year.'

Since graduated to Glory, Zola Levit's "Introduction to Hebrew," is informative:

What's in a Name?

The relation between a name (shem) and a thing (davar) is of fundamental importance in the Scriptures. In the Hebraic mindset, 'naming' and 'being' are linked together to form a 'unity'. The right use of a name denotes a right relationship with the thing named, as Adam established dominion over the creatures of the earth by giving them their names (see Gen. 2:19).

Once again, the careful scholar is reminded of God's attention to priority as daily work halts to pay tribute to eternal schedules above the mundane workaday involvements.

Malachi

God's final revelation, before His silence, is bestowed to the prophet Malachi. In this closing prophecy the Lord again proclaims one last time the Lord's return to earth.

"Behold, I send my messenger, and he will prepare the way before me. And the Lord, whom you seek, will <u>suddenly</u> come to His temple..." {Malachi 3:1, ESV}

Malachi goes on to speak of the day of the Lord. God's promise of Elijah returning before that great day is proclaimed. Jesus spoke of John the Baptist coming in Elijah's spirit. Yet many rejected John the Baptist.

Thus, Elijah himself shall return before that day, and possibly be one of the two Revelation witnesses that are martyred mid-way through the Tribulation. Intriguingly, the second may well be Enoch, another prophet who was translated alive to God. Note these prophets shall be martyred and then shall rise after three days!

For our concerns, it is enough for now to know the Lord's confirmation of His Return _with_ His saints! The Rapture at that point having already been enacted.

Now, let us thus enter our study of the Brit Chadashah, the New Covenant, the New Testament, and our Blessed Hope.

With an eye on the clock we shall leapfrog the momentous annunciation and birth of Ha Maschiach as God breaks His silence of four centuries with the birth announcement of Immanuel.

Chapter Six

The Olivet Discourses – Rapture Portions

---

a.d. 30-33–Olivet Discourses–Rapture references
a.d. 55-65 Matthew
a.d. 55-65 Mark
a.d. 55-65 Luke
a.d. 55-65 John

P hilip Comfort, in his seminal study of the formation of
the New Testament, *'Encountering the Manuscripts,'*
strives to clarify the three levels of written Gospels that
developed following Jesus' initial oral proclamations
during His public ministry, circa a.d. 30-33. These would
comprise the writings that eventually became the flower
of the Christian canon.

Comfort first determines the initial oral proclamations that began with Jesus in his public ministry that
would supply the foundations of the Four Gospels of the
Brit Chadashah (New Testament).

He simultaneously bridges back to the Tanakh.
Comfort then introduces a.d. 49 as the earliest known

date of published New Testament writings recorded as of the publication of his book. (pg. 11, B&H Academic, November 15, 2005)

He examines extant fragments of parchment scrolls that establish the original individual autographs resulting from the oral messages. Comfort continues to the second stage that emerges by the beginning of the second century, i.e., a.d. 101, revealing the collections of groupings including *'the four Gospels and Paul's major epistles.'* {Pages 11-12}

The canon of Scripture formed into the New Testament in its entirety would be completed by the early 4th century, i.e., c. a.d.300's.

Oral proclamation at the beginning of the first century is deemed the first tier of publication, as emphasized by Comfort. This bears witness to the legitimacy of Jesus' preaching to public audiences. Matt. 7:29 records, "For He taught them as one having authority, and not as the scribes," further elevating and 'Divining' His messages. {KJV}

An obvious first New Testament time-glimpse of the Rapture, chronologically then, materializes within the oral traditions of both the synoptic Gospels, *Matthew*, *Mark*, and *Luke*, and the often referenced *'spiritual' Gospel of John.* The major passages appear through what has become known down through the ages as 'the 'Olivet Discourse',

Among many scholars Matthew is traditionally earmarked as the initial Gospel transcribed to scroll, c. a.d. 50-69. Although the Gospel of Mark, according to some, vies for first transcription, at this point in time, tradition generally attributes Mark to the second publication of the four. Luke and Acts are ascribed to the same era, as is the

Gospel of John* roughly in the same period. * *(See editor's note opening the Gospel of John passage, pg. 90)*

Matthew

Delving then into Jesus' focusing on the imminent Rapture in the Gospels, one enters a minefield of objections by many Christians concerning references to our 'Blessed Hope.

Perhaps the first authoritative passage that needs to be proclaimed establishing the reality and existence of the church itself is Jesus' declaration to Peter in Matt. 16:17-18:

> *"17 And Jesus answered and said unto him, Blessed art thou, Simon Bar-jona: for flesh and blood hath not revealed it unto thee, but my Father which is in heaven. 18 And I say also unto thee, That thou art Peter, and upon this rock, *(The rock being* **Peter's profession of faith that Jesus is the Messiah/Christ, not Peter himself, and that faith in Jesus, being Messiah, the rock** *...), I will build my church; and the gates of hell shall not prevail against it." Au-KJV*

*{Of course, entire denominations have been built on the different interpretations of meaning in this verse. And, to be fair, I have input my understanding. But the focusing point in this study is that here Jesus, in this passage, establishes the reality of the church, thus including specifically, all believers in any preparatory references He makes to the 'imminent Rapture and all consequential results.}

Focusing on the specific prophecy of the imminent Rapture then, even among those who otherwise accept the pre-Millennial, pre-Tribulation, imminent Rapture prophecy posture, as taught in the epistles and letters of Paul and other writers, varying views persist as to any personal mention of the event by Jesus.

Of these, some attest to the belief that Jesus does speak to the Rapture, others that Jesus does so rarely, while the majority of professing believers throughout Christendom do not even acknowledge the prophecy itself of our Blessed Hope being legitimate.

In Matthew Chapters' 24 & 25, for example, some objectors insist Jesus is only speaking to the Jews about Jewish end-time events, that He is not speaking to the Church at all. This group demands that our Lord never refers to the Shout in any way in this Gospel.

These protestors' objections melt away in the face of Jesus' request in His prayer in John 17:20-23:

"20 Neither pray I for these alone, but for them also which shall believe on me through their word; 21 that they all may be one; as thou, Father, art in me, and I in thee, that they also may be one in us: that the world may believe that thou hast sent me. 22 And the glory which thou gavest me I have given them; that they may be one, even as we are one: 23 I in them, and thou in me, that they may be made perfect in one; and that the world may know that thou hast sent me, and hast loved them, as thou hast loved me." Au-KJV

Note Jesus acknowledging future believers through the words of the disciples. Then He reasons that 'all may be one' even as Jesus and the Father are one. (Parenthetically, no mention is made of the Holy Spirit because Jesus instructed the Comforter would not speak of Himself.) Emphasis is added that all may be one in Jesus and the Father, a union that will confirm to the world the Father has indeed sent Jesus.

In addition, a close study of portions of Matthew 24 & 25, in adhering to Jesus' admonition to rightly divide the word, clearly intimate the foreshadowing of His promised Shout for His Bride prophesied in the epistles and letters of the New Testament.

As Chapter 24 opens, Jesus departs from the Temple. His disciples point out the magnificence of the structure. Jesus declares a time coming when 'there shall not be left here one stone upon another, that shall not be thrown down.' Verses :1-2, Au-KJV

Jesus then climbs to the mount of Olives where Matthew picks up the narrative:

"...as he sat upon the mount of Olives, the disciples came unto him privately, saying, tell us..." 1) when shall these things be (the destruction of the Temple)? 2) And what shall be the sign of thy coming? 3) and of the end of the world?"

Markedly, Jesus first warns against deception. A warning he emphasizes twice more in the next few verses. Pointedly then, are there any among us who would claim they can easily see the truth in this day and age? Even Paul, in his day conceded in this life we see through a glass darkly.

"12 For now we see through a glass, darkly; but then face to face: now I know in part; but then

shall I know even as also I am known." {I Cor. 13:12, Au-KJV}

Jesus highlights forms of deception and distraction as: false messiahs gaining followers, even claiming they are Jesus Himself; wars; rumors of wars; none of which He emphasizes should trouble believers because all these 'MUST come to pass, but the end is not yet.'

Jesus includes famines, pestilences, earthquakes in 'divers' (diverse) places.

Incredibly, when a series of major earthquakes began activating around the world within days of each other this last decade, a seismologist was commissioned to find any relation between these natural catastrophes. Following a months-long study, he insisted 'no connection.' Asked how he could be so certain, he replied, "Because these quakes were all in 'diverse' places." He was unaware of quoting verbatim from the 1611 King James Bible version, Matthew 24:7, "… and earthquakes, in diverse places …"

In Matthew 24:30, responding to the 'sign' question, the reader discovers Jesus prophesying, "… [30] and then shall appear the sign of the Son of man in heaven: and then shall all the tribes of the earth mourn, and they shall see the Son of man coming in the clouds of heaven with power and great glory. [31] And he shall send his angels with a great sound of a trumpet, and they shall gather together his elect from the four winds, from one end of heaven to the other." No confusion here. A clear declaration the world shall see Jesus 'coming in the clouds of heaven with power and great glory.'

Some would grasp at verse 31, which reveals Jesus sending His angels with a sounding trumpet to gather

His elect from the four winds, from one end of heaven to the other.

Yet Jesus interjects immediately the parable of the fig tree and its yearly gestation in the spring, emphasizing the end-times happenings He has been describing shall *'begin'* in this blossoming time, continuing throughout this season to the fruition of 'all' these things in complete fulfillment. And at the 'budding', the end shall <u>begin</u> to draw near ... but not yet.

He has revealed that He shall appear as lightening in His return to earth, yet here begins to describe an unknown day and hour reminiscent of the days of Noe, in which life was continuing as it had from the beginning. And folks unmindfully remained in total ignorance 'until the flood came.' Once the rain began, the deluge only abated when all life outside the ark was destroyed. There at least will be life when Jesus returns at this juncture <u>with</u> His Bride, per Revelation 19.

Overemphasis should not be feared that the Lord likens this unknown event to that of a 'thief' breaking in, mirroring Paul's I Thess. 5:2 conclusion in describing our imminent elopement with Jesus.

Beginning then with the oral tradition in Matt. 24:37 Jesus hearkens back to the days of *Noah* to parallel those similarities in society that mirror the end of days and the coming of the Son of Man. Jesus leads the listener through Noahic era activities, i.e., eating, drinking, marrying and giving in marriage. All of these practices being enacted as Noah proclaims the coming judgment of God while busying himself building the ark.

Everyone on earth, ignoring Noah's preaching, is oblivious to the approaching destruction of all life as they know it. Then Jesus says, "...until the day that

Noah entered into the ark." One is hard pressed to ignore the microscopic exactness in timing as Jesus speaks of "the day."

Jesus notes their oblivion was completed as the flood came and took away all those alive who had rejected Noah's warnings (they all died).

Continuing on, Jesus then outlines the foreshadowing of the Rapture. Just as certain as that report of the world-wide flood given in Genesis is Jesus' prophecy of the imminent Rapture. He continues:

> "Then shall two be in the field; the one shall be taken, and the other left. Two women shall be grinding at the mill; the one shall be taken, and the other left. Watch therefore: for ye know not what hour your Lord doth come. But know this that if the Goodman of the house had known in what watch the thief would come, he would have watched, and would not have suffered his house to be broken up. Therefore, be ye also ready: for in such an hour as ye think not the Son of man cometh." {Matt. 24:40-44, KJV}

This passage's reference to the disappearances has been linked by some Bible scholars to Tribulation deaths. Others connect this prophecy of the disappearances or vanishings instead with the Rapture.

First, note that '…one shall be taken, and the other left.' 'Taken' is defined in Strong's Exhaustive Concordance of the Bible as, "…*par-al-am-ban'-o; from 3844 and 2983; to receive near, i.e. associate with oneself (in any familiar or intimate act or relation): by analogy to assume an office; figurative to learn; -receive, take (unto, with).*"

There is not only no suggestion of death in 'taken', which violates the context, factually the definition reveals the action to be one of deliverance unto promotion.

More importantly the inclusion of the 'thief' in verse 43 dovetails into Paul's I Thess. 5:4 description of 'that day' overtaking the unobservant as a 'thief.' This alignment also couples with Paul's II Thess. 2:3 clarification of the saints' departure prior to the revelation of the Anti-Christ.

Remember Jesus has earlier described the abomination of desolation that would take place in the temple and a period of time to follow that would not only eclipse any previous historical catastrophes, but would never be overshadowed in the future, "... or ever shall be."

Notice the similarity between these people being taken away *en masse* in an unidentifiable moment, the previous, equally mysterious disappearance of Enoch, and the prophesied catching away in I Thess. 4:13-14. Striking wouldn't you say? Vanished. Without a trace.

Mark also Jesus' warning to the goodman of the house that a thief is coming 'in an hour that ye think not.' And there are those who are left behind, apportioned suffering with the hypocrites, with weeping and gnashing of teeth.

Again, roughly two decades on, the Apostle Paul reiterates the warning of the beginning of the Day of the Lord, in I Thess. 5:2, being prefaced by Jesus coming 'as a thief in the night' to the unbelieving. Remember, Jesus warns He will appear as a thief to those unprepared. Paul echoes the distinction in verse four of the aforementioned Thessalonian passage when he remarks, "But ye, brethren, are not in darkness, that that day should overtake you as a thief." This also underscores Jesus' warning to 'watch.' {KJV}

So, Paul is emphasizing the season of the Rapture will become obvious, though the moment of the event itself will be impossible to establish without a super-ultra-high-speed camera!

Please also be reminded this is a study of the imminence of the Rapture, which initiates the Day of the Lord, itself a teaching meriting exam of its own. As Jesus pointed out in 24:44 of the Olivet passage we have just been considering, "Therefore be ye also ready: for in such an hour as ye think not the Son of man cometh." {KJV}

This warning has to be in reference to the imminent or any moment Rapture because, first of all, Jesus likens the Rapture for the unprepared as the coming of a thief that breaks in and escapes with valuables. Because of Jesus' instructions, Paul reminds believers in I Thess. 5:4-5 that He will not be coming as a thief to them, because as sons of light, believers "...are not of darkness..."

Already, in this same monologue, Jesus has spoken of His Return to the earth itself as lightening flashing from the East to the West. These visuals alert the reader to the world-wide witness of His coming to earth itself. {Matt. 24:27}

Additionally, John declares in Rev. 1:7 '...every eye shall see Him...' when Jesus returns to this earth. Evidently it will have to include world-wide media coverage. Not an inconspicuous, unobservable or unannounced entrance this!

But we digress. Returning to the imminence of the Rapture we find Jesus continuing in the Olivet discourse of Matthew with the parable of the ten virgins. "And while they (the five foolish) went to buy (oil), the bridegroom came; and they that were ready went in with him to the marriage: and the door was shut." {Matt. 25:10, KJV}

Shocking, wouldn't you say? But not without warning. Notice also the phraseology Jesus uses. Remember He had earlier referenced Noah. In the Genesis 7:16 passage we read, "And they that went in, went in male and female of all flesh, as God had commanded him: and the LORD shut him in." 'Shut' is 'shut' in both the Hebrew of the Tanakh and in the Greek of the Brit Chadashah. Both times those on the outside are barred from entering in. And there is weeping and gnashing of teeth without. {NASB}

Keeping oil in your lamp was not merely a daily chore in that day, to use the lamp after dark, it had to be kept ready into the night, especially if one was *anticipating* an imminent need before sunrise!

Conversely, if you don't believe in imminent need, why be concerned? Right? There would be plenty of time while witnessing His return from the sky.

The disciple whom Jesus loved emphasized this anticipation in I John 3:3. "And every man that hath this hope in him purifieth himself, even as he is pure." Note the individual, personal responsibility here in the phrase "...every man..." And the word 'hope,' translated from the Greek in Strong's 1680, reads "...elpis, el-pece'; from a prim. 'Elpo' (to anticipate, with pleasure); expectation (abstr. Or concr.) Or confidence: -faith, hope." {KJV}

In fact, Jesus continues His Olivet sermon following up the description of the Rapture by then declaring personal responsibility through His parable of the talents.

Each man is responsible for the talents given him only. And having even only one talent does not reduce one's personal responsibility. In fact, Jesus declares those refusing to use whatever talents they might have, large or small, will be counted unworthy to remain in

His presence and shall also be cast into outer darkness where there will again be weeping and gnashing of teeth. Significantly, Divine Judgment is eternal, not a superficial, momentary experience.

Jesus' words in Luke 21:36, "...that ye may be accounted *worthy*..." ring more stridently when considered with the parable of the talents. {KJV}

Again, cutting edge prophecy is revealed. Parenthetically, one can easily see the importance of grasping the significance of the imminence of the Rapture laid against its proclamation.

It, the imminent Rapture, is not some mere child's bedtime story to soothe the troubled babes as they lay themselves down to sleep. Men's hearts are going to begin failing them as earth's turmoil accelerates. The comfort and strengthening bestowed through the anticipation of His any moment deliverance shall lift the hearts of all who believe. {Luke 21:26}

Moreover, some risk losing the reward of a crown by neglecting the anticipation of this blessed event.

Others squander their opportunity to escape the Tribulation because they are not yet saved. The loss of Heaven and the Lord will be the greatest tragedy. Great multitudes that spurn God's invitation to salvation even during the Tribulation, shall lose Heaven eternally and fall to the never-ending Hell. They shall not only lose the Rapture prophesied, but eternally greater, God's free gift of redemption.

Mark

We now approach Mark 13 for the beginning of the Olivet Discourse, which is initiated as Jesus and the disciples are leaving the Temple area for the Mount of Olives.

This passage contains many of the elements of the Matthew sermon, and also finishes with a reference to the Rapture.

Leaving the Temple, Jesus is encouraged by one of the disciples to consider the magnificence of the architecture and stones of the buildings on its' grounds. The Lord acknowledges first the buildings are indeed great while yet then prophesying not even one stone will one day be left upon another, but all shall be thrown down.

Robert Cornuke, in his excellent work, 'Temple', emphasizes the fact that if the 'Temple Mount' in Jerusalem were the true site of Jesus' prophecy there would be no 'wailing wall' with stones still 'left one stone upon another.' Without digressing, all are encouraged to examine his study on Zion and the actual Temple-site in David's City.

Sitting on the Mount of Olives, "… over against the temple. Peter and James, and John and Andrew …" ask Jesus privately, "… when shall these things be, and what shall be the sign when all these shall be fulfilled." {Mark 13:3, KJV}

Near the end of the discourse, in 13:32-33, Jesus warns, "But of that day and that hour knoweth no man, no, not the angels which are in heaven, neither the Son, but the Father. Take ye heed, watch and pray: for ye know not when the time is." {KJV}

His personal addressing of the perfectly described event of the Rapture heightens the impact of the prophecy to the nth degree ... And central to His warning is the imminence.

Per example, interjecting the parable of the fig tree into his discourse on end time events, Jesus concludes with the following admonition:

"[30] Verily I say unto you, that this generation shall not pass, till all these things be done. [31] Heaven and earth shall pass away: but my words shall not pass away.

"[32] But of that day and *that* hour knoweth no man, no, not the angels which are in heaven, neither the Son, but the Father. [33] Take ye heed, watch and pray: for ye know not when the time is. [34] *For the Son of man is* as a man taking a far journey, who left his house, and gave authority to his servants, and to every man his work, and commanded the porter to watch.

"[35] Watch ye therefore: for ye know not when the master of the house cometh, at even, or at midnight, or at the cockcrowing, or in the morning: [36]lest coming suddenly he find you sleeping. [37]And what I say unto you I say unto all, Watch." {13:30-37, Au-KJV}

Here Jesus accentuates strongly, '... I say unto ALL ...'

Hidden within this heightened stress explodes the 'imminence' of His promised 'Shout.' *All* who believe in Jesus down through the ages to the present are enjoined to 'watch.' !!!

It is also noteworthy here to recognize the similarity between this passage and the Acts 1 admonition that none shall know 'the day or the hour.' Yet unlike the Mark verses, the Acts admonition points to the Return of Jesus to the earth for the restoration of the kingdom to Israel. But these Mark verses speak of the days leading to the pre-Tribulation snatching of the Church, (seven years prior to Rev. 19 and Jesus' return to earth with His Bride).

For Jesus speaks in Chapter 13 of the wrath of God that shall first befall the world and all nations, Israel, and Tribulation believers in particular. Paul, however, refined the perspective with assurance that the Thessalonian believers are not appointed unto wrath. Believers are appointed unto deliverance, escape and evacuation out of the trials that shall come upon the whole earth. So, the reader catches a glimpse in Mark of those saved in the Tribulation, but not out of it.

More largely, the future rests on David's petition in Ps. 31:15, "My times are in your hand; deliver me from the hand of my enemies, and from those who persecute me." Thus, in the New Testament God reveals the greatest delivery imaginable. For those who believe. {NKJV}

Therefore, the warning that none can know the day and the hour is used by Jesus in this passage to emphasize the importance of watching! Jesus doesn't say, since no one knows the day or the hour there is no need to be concerned with the timing of the prophecy. Rather Jesus demands in the imperative that for that very reason, the closer the prophecies begin to gather, such as earthquakes, wars, rumors of wars, etc., the more vigilant believers must become. {Matt. 24:6}

Again, the student of scripture understands that Daniel has prophesied the number of days totaling the time of Jacob's trouble, also called the Tribulation. Though during the Tribulation, the Anti-Christ strives to change the times and seasons for his own purposes, the observant during those days will be able to track the fulfillment of all prophecies **nearly** to the very day of Jesus' return to earth at the end of the Tribulation.

"Nearly" is as close as anyone will be able to estimate the time of the end of the Tribulation and Jesus' physical return to the earth. Because the Anti-Christ, "… will try to change their sacred festivals and laws…" Thinking he is in control of all things, the Anti-Christ will change the calendar because it, for one, stands at 'anno domini' (in the year of our Lord). From that point at the mid-Tribulation, it will become arduous for the unprepared to keep track of the exact duration of the Tribulation as it continues to unfold. {Dan. 7:25, NLT}

One time-piece for tracking will be the event Jesus notes as 'the abomination of desolation' at the halfway mark of the seven years.

And, of course, at the end when from the moment Jesus appears, by His own description, as lightening from the East to the West, the world will know He is back, indeed every eye shall see Him!

Yet, again returning to His imminent Shout, Mark 13:36 reveals some shall be found unmindful of the master's coming for His Bride before the Tribulation begins, "Lest coming suddenly he find you sleeping." {KJV}

Which hearkens back to Jesus' allusion in the Parable of the Talents when warning the lord of the house will surely return. And Matthew's five sleeping virgins are caught at midnight without oil for their lamps. Thus, those watching must be careful not to be caught sleeping spiritually lest He come suddenly, (imminently – at any moment), as a thief!

So here in Mark 13:35-36, Jesus once again emphasizes no man knows the day or the hour, citing the fact that "…you do not know when the Master of the house is coming—in the evening, at midnight, at the crowing of the rooster, or in the morning—lest coming suddenly, he finds you sleeping." In this context, Jesus is referring to the imminent coming for His Bride. {KJV}

God is not against people getting needed sleep. In fact, Psalm 127:2 reveals the exact opposite. "It is in vain that you rise up early and go late to rest, eating the bread of anxious toil; for he gives to his beloved sleep." {ESV}

Countless times this author has called to the Lord to still his heart to sleep, and God has always been faithful. The Good Shepherd gives His beloved sheep the rest they require. Then why would this Mark passage warn against sleeping? The Holy Spirit is emphasizing the imminence! Anticipation cultivates the fixed under-standing that the expected event is coming any moment on a day that *must* be called 'today'!

As believers gain the understanding of Jesus calling out His Bride at any moment, knowing they will be ready to hear His Shout, even in a dead sleep! It is the unbe-lieving that will allow themselves to be overcome with surfeiting, drunkenness and the cares of this world that will suffer the rudest awakening in history!

One final note demands entrance. The closing verse of Mark 13:37 reveals the inclusion of all who believe in Jesus, present and future. And, yes, Jesus speaks directly to the anticipation of the Rapture, warning all believers to take heed of this most blessed of promises.

Jesus is obviously speaking to his disciples. But Mark 13 closes with Jesus categorically emphasizing that every believer take heed to this proclamation, when he states, unequivocally, "³⁷ And what I say unto you, (the disci-ples there listening, I say unto *all*, Watch."

Two points are being emphasized by the Lord, here. All believers are included in this warning, and the moment of escape is 'imminent' and shall activate at any atom-smashing Shout in the 24-hour period.

Jesus begins with 'evening' because God inspired the description of the creation's six days as, "… and evening and morning were the *first* day."

Luke

Moving to Luke 12:35-48 we find Jesus again offering the parable of the master of the house returning undeclared as a thief. But where Jesus has previously spoken of the day and the hour, now He emphasizes the hour alone.

> *"But know this that if the master of the house had known what hour the thief would come, he would have watched and not allowed his house to be broken into. Therefore, you also be ready, for the Son of Man is coming at an hour you do not expect." {Luke 12:39-40, NKJV}*

Peter then asks, vs. 41, "Lord, do You speak this parable *only* to us, or to all *people?*"

Jesus' petition to His Father in John 17:20 immediately comes to the fore. "Neither pray I for these alone, but for them also which shall believe on me through their word;" And again His pronouncement in Mark 13:37, as Jesus encapsulates that Olivet discourse, finishing by describing the parable of the Rapture, "[37] And what I say unto you I say unto all, Watch." {Au-KJV; NKJV}

Discerning observers realize this necessitates those personally watching be sensitive not only for each day,

but even for each hour. Luke writes, "...*is* coming..."
Again, the 'imminence' rises.

And now turning to Luke Chapter 21:33-36 the reader
discovers Jesus, having again been documenting the end
days and time of Jacob's trouble, finalizing the tableaux
by exclaiming, "Heaven and earth shall pass away; but
my words shall not pass away." {KJV}

Not trying to put the cart before the horse, we understand that there will be according to Revelation 21:1 a
new Heaven and a new Earth, because the first Heaven
and the first Earth have passed away. "Then I saw a new
heaven and a new earth, for the first heaven and the first
earth had passed away, and the sea was no more." {ESV}

But here, Jesus capitalizes on this astounding prophecy
to galvanize His listeners to focus on what He is telling
them, as he continues in verses 34-36:

> *"Take heed to yourselves, lest at any time your
> hearts be overcharged with surfeiting, and drunk-
> enness, and cares of this life, and so that day come
> upon you unawares. For as a snare shall it come
> on all them that dwell on the whole earth. Watch
> ye therefore, and pray always, that ye may be
> accounted worthy to escape all these things that
> shall come to pass, and to stand before the Son of
> man." {Luke 21:34-36, KJV}*

First of all, 'surfeiting' is overindulging! Jesus adds in
the very next moment 'drunkenness.' Then He includes
the cares of this life. That could be anything that captures you, whether it is sin, or just the overindulgence of
the innocent pleasures of this life. Per example, are you
a workaholic?

Truly, in a telling testimony, during a missionary discussion of overwork, one participant in the midst of the meeting suddenly sat bolt upright and proclaimed emphatically, "I can put the pencil down!" Pointedly, there had been no comments directed toward him personally to that moment. His conviction of losing sight of the Master in the midst of service was apparent.

Yet the speed of the activating Rapture reveals our calling out shall yank us even before we can 'put the pencil down'!!!

Jesus' warning also contains a concealed blessing as one is easily reminded of Is. 26:3, "You keep him in perfect peace whose mind is stayed on you, because he trusts in you." A verse that begins and ends with God, this passage guides the believer into the complete peace of God. A promise without limit, the verse also includes direction for the mind while simultaneously blessing those who trust in God for doing so. {ESV}

Continuing with Luke 21:36 Jesus nails the Rapture. He has already prefigured the imminence when He prophesies that the abrupt start of the Tribulation is going to come upon the world as a snare. Therefore, He is commanding His followers to watch in order that they may *escape* this snare.

The escape is the Rapture. The use of this term '*escape*' exposes yet once more, the imminent aspect of timing! Thus, the 'escape' of the event describes the suddenness of the timing.

John

Now we come to what has been famously described as 'the spiritual Gospel.' 'The Gospel of John' is first of all unlike the first three Gospels in the New Testament, which are *synoptic* and patterned similarly, viewing many of the same events, espousing much of the same biography and life of Jesus. In this Gospel the Holy Spirit departs from the previous leading and moves John to write about the very person of Jesus and who He is eternally.

Talk about reverting to the chase! Not coincidentally, John 1:1 mirror's the opening of the Tanakh, Gen. 1:1, "In the beginning God created the heavens and the earth." "In the beginning was the Word, and the Word was with God, and the Word was God." {NIV}

John completes the revelation in John 1:14, "And the Word was made flesh, and dwelt among us, (and we beheld his glory, the glory as of the only begotten of the Father,) full of grace and truth." {KJV}

This coupling is significant for the authority it affords the two passages we shall consider in contemplating the imminent Rapture.

*{Here, in the 'Blast Off' Gospel narrative, a major 'time' re-configuring must take place.

Because our focus is centered on the timing of the Rapture, and this ensuing work thus strives to gain a chronological perspective of the development of the revelation of the prophesying of our Blessed Hope, further study has demanded we submit to the leading of Scripture.

In previous editions we had attributed the writing of John's Gospel to after the Book of Revelation, at the close of the 1ˢᵗ Century, as the apostle's final work.

However, in his Gospel, John clearly settles the timing of the writing of this Gospel as before the destruction of Jerusalem in 70 a.d.

*"² Now there **is** at Jerusalem by the sheep market a pool, which **is** called in the Hebrew tongue Bethesda, having five porches." John 5:2, KJV*

*Note John's placement of personal view in the present tense, "Now there **is** ... which **is** called ...". Thus, recorded in the 'present' tense, the reader realizes the writer's ignoring the mention of the Roman destruction of Jerusalem setting that historical event as 'yet future'. Had the destruction already been accomplished, the phrase would have read 'Now there **was** ... which **was** called ...' Author's note.}*

In 5:25-29, Jesus offers both encouragement and warning in what may be references to both the Rapture and His earthly return.

"²⁵ Verily, verily, I say unto you, The hour is coming, and now is, when the dead shall hear the voice of the Son of God: and they that hear shall live. ²⁶ For as the Father hath life in himself; so hath he given to the Son to have life in himself; ²⁷ and hath given him authority to execute judgment also, because he is the Son of man. ²⁸ Marvel not at this: for the hour is coming, in the which all that are in the graves shall hear his voice, ²⁹ and shall come forth; they that have done good, unto the resurrection of life; and they that have done evil, unto the resurrection of damnation." {Au-KJV}

In 5:25 Jesus speaks of the dead being resurrected unto life at the Rapture. In 5:28-29, Jesus speaks to the dead being resurrected to both rewards and damnation. Perfect silhouettes of the Rapture and then, those resurrected later to final judgment.

Note that Paul later clarifies *'the dead in Christ shall rise first.'* That shall leave many not resurrected, including all who die during the Tribulation.

Lazarus dies, Chapter 11, and Jesus is confronted by Martha, then Mary.

John 11:25-26 reads, "Jesus said to her, 'I am the resurrection and the life. He who believes in Me, though he may die, he shall live. And whoever lives and believes in Me shall never die. Do you believe this?'" {NKJV}

Lazarus has died. Martha, who first complained because Mary was sitting at the feet of Jesus instead of helping with chores, hears Jesus is on His way to their house and rushes to meet Him. Martha greets Jesus with, "Lord, if You had been here, my brother would not have died." {11:21, NKJV}

To be fair to Martha, Mary too would accost Jesus with that identical challenge that Lazarus would still be alive if Jesus had been present. Notwithstanding Mary had been commended by Jesus earlier for her singular devotion to Him.

As Jesus discusses Lazarus with Martha, in context, He begins to expound and expand on His own person, declaring He is the resurrection and the life, and that whoever believes in Him, though they die, yet shall they live. Then Jesus continues, declaring those who live who believe in Him shall never die. Paul echoes these very words in I Cor. 15:51, "Listen, I tell you a mystery: We will not all sleep (die), but we will all be changed..." {NIV}

Jesus is not telling Martha only that when someone is resurrected, they shall never again die. He is expanding His revelation to now declare that there are some who believe in Him that shall never die even once! This is the beginning of the mystery revelation that Paul exposes to the Corinthians. This is an essential part of the doctrine of the imminent Rapture.

Again, Jesus says, "…And whoever lives and believes in Me shall never die." Paul proclaimed, "…then we which are alive and remain shall be caught up (violently snatched away in Divine ecstasy) together with them (the dead who have just been resurrected) in the clouds, to meet the Lord in the air: and so shall we ever be with the Lord."

Paul goes on in verse 52 of I Cor. 15, "In a moment, in the twinkling of an eye, at the last trump: for the trumpet shall sound, and the dead shall be raised incorruptible, and we shall be changed." {KJV}

There it is again, in a moment, in the twinkling of an eye, in 11/100ths of a second, we who are alive and remain shall be changed and caught up, violently snatched away, again as properly understood, in Divine ecstasy!

Death is a horrible enemy, as described by Paul in 1 Cor. 15:26, and shall be the last enemy slain by God! "The last enemy *that* shall be destroyed *is* death." {KJV}

Yet even before Jesus destroys death there are some of us that shall escape death through the Rapture! As Paul, in I Cor. 15:55, quotes in paraphrase Hos. 13:14, "O Death, where is your sting? O Hades, where is your victory?" {NKJV}

Thus, Isaiah rejoices, "He will swallow up death in victory…" {Isaiah 25:8, American King James Version}

But can you rejoice despite your own death? Jesus did. Hebrews 12:2, "...looking to Jesus, the founder and perfecter of our faith, who for the joy that was set before him endured the cross, despising the shame, and is seated at the right hand of the throne of God." {ESV}

More than this, in John 14:1-3, at His last Passover supper, on His way to certain death, Jesus comforted Peter. Jesus had just contradicted Peter's vow that he would lay down his life for Jesus. Jesus corrects Peter, explaining Peter would deny Him three times that night before the cock crowed twice!

So then, transporting to the Gospel of John 14:1, written before the Roman destruction of Jerusalem in 70 a.d. and the dispersion of the Jews, we find one of the most dramatic announcements recorded in the Brit Chadashah.

At the end of the chapter, 13:38, Jesus reveals Peter is going to deny Him three times that very night. The chapter break was inserted over a millennium later.*

*The Chapter Headings Were Added in the Thirteenth Century:

A man named Stephen Langton divided the Bible into chapters in the year A.D. 1227.
Langton was a professor at the University of Paris, later elevated to Archbishop of Canterbury.

The Verse Enumerations Were Added in the Sixteenth Century:

Robert Stephanus (Stephens), a French printer, divided the verses for his Greek New Testament. It was published in 1551.

The First Bible with Chapter And Verse Divisions:

The first entire Bible in which these chapter and verse divisions were used was Stephen's edition of the Latin Vulgate (1555). The first English New Testament to have both chapter and verse divisions was the Geneva Bible (1560). Fortunately, Jewish scholars have followed the way of dividing the Hebrew Scripture into chapters and verses. (blueletterbible.org)

This revelation to Peter must be received in light of Jesus' personal awareness of the approach of horrific agonies He would begin to suffer this very night. Yet overriding even the impending crucifixion is the Divine reality that Jesus is the Truth.

Thus John 14:1 is a continuation of the ending of the previous chapter, 13:38. Having divulged this devastating betrayal by Peter, Jesus immediately begins to comfort him by encouraging him first in his faith in God and then to have faith in Jesus Himself. He explains that in His Father's house are many mansions, and that He is in fact going away to prepare a place for Peter. By extension it is understood that this promise is for all believers. "Neither pray I for these alone, but for them also which shall believe on me through their word..." {John 17:20, KJV}

Jesus continues in verse 3, "And if I go and prepare a place for you, I will come again, and receive you unto myself; that where I am, there ye may be also." The use of 'ye' directs the statement to Peter personally, because at that point Peter needed personal encouragement. Accordingly, then, this is a foreshadowing of the personal promise to each of us 'in Christ.' {KJV}

He would need this strengthening even more after his denial of Jesus, when the Lord looks Peter directly in the eye following the third denial.

> *Luke 22:60-61, KJV, witnesses, "And Peter said, 'Man, I know not what thou sayest.' And immediately, while he yet spake, the cock crew. And the Lord turned and looked upon Peter. And Peter remembered the word of the Lord, how He had said to him…"*

> *"I tell you the truth, Peter – this very night, before the rooster crows twice, you will deny three times that you even know me." {Mark 14:30, NLT}*

'And the Lord turned, and looked upon Peter,' exposing the necessity of Peter being prepared for the shock of denying his Lord through prior strengthening. The same uplifting is recorded when Paul, in I Thess. 5:11, encourages and commends the brethren for edifying and strengthening one another with the doctrine of this same imminent Rapture prophecy.

For Jesus, in 14:3, has assured Peter that He will *receive* Peter *unto* Himself. Although Jesus is promising Peter of His return, Jesus is distinguishing this return by emphasizing that He will *receive* Peter unto Himself, He will draw Peter to Himself, in the identical manner in which a King receives His audience into His presence.

The King does not come to his subject (on the earth), rather His subject comes to Him (in the air).

This coincides with Paul's Thessalonian description of the event in which the dead in Christ rise and then '…we who are alive and remain shall be *caught up* (<u>violently snatched in divine ecstasy</u>) together with them in the clouds…"

And as Jesus told Peter, "…*receive you to myself* …" All we, dead and alive, shall be Royally Summoned by Jesus Himself!

As Peter stood there dumbfounded, Jesus then comforted the impetuous disciple, "Let not your heart be troubled: ye believe in God, believe also in me. In my Father's house are many mansions: if *it were* not *so*, I would have told you. I go to prepare a place for you. And if I go and prepare a place for you, I will come again, and receive you unto myself; that where I am, *there* ye may be also." {John 14:1-3, KJV}

In His own words Jesus comforts with the promise that He will come again and *receive* Peter. Peter will go to Him. The dead in Christ will rise first. In retrospect, we now know Peter's body will be among those dead bodies in Christ that shall rise first to be reunited with their eternal spirits to meet Jesus in the air! And where are we all going?

Jesus explains to Peter that where Jesus shall be, so Peter and all believers will be also, *eve*r to be with the Lord! Now that is strength for the journey plus comfort!

It has ever been so that Jesus keeps the best for last. So, as He does with Peter, He also finishes the book of Revelation. He reveals in His closing words of Chapter 22:20, the importance of keeping uppermost in our minds the imminent Rapture, "[20] He which testifieth these things saith, 'Surely I come quickly.'" Au-KJV

If ever there were a doctrine in all of Scripture that has created divisions, arguments, and outright controversy, it is the doctrine of the Return of Jesus, and how it will play out. But then, Jesus Himself declared, "Do not think that I came to bring peace on the earth; I did not come to bring peace, but a sword." {Matt. 10:34, NASB}

Chapter Seven

First Written Rapture Teachings

⸻⸻◦⸻⸻

a.d. 45-50–James
a.d. 48-58 – Galatians
a.d. 51—I Thessalonians

Following Jesus' ascension into Heaven, (Acts 1:9), He birthed the Church through God the Holy Spirit {Acts 2:1-4, a.d. 33}.

The work of God in Jesus to build His Church began with the anointing earnest of the Holy Spirit. "Who hath also sealed us and given the earnest of the Spirit in our hearts." {II Cor. 1:22, KJV}

All of the witnessing to the death, burial and resurrection of Jesus, through preaching, praying and fellowshipping of the saints thus began.

The first three recorded writings that emerged, according to much considered, biblical, historical scholarship, were an epistle from Jesus' half-brother, James, circa a.d. 45-50; followed by two Pauline letters addressed to a new congregation in Thessalonica in a.d. 51.

Several verses come to mind as we begin to consider the written documentation of the Rapture teaching. Most importantly, "All Scripture is God-breathed and is useful for teaching, rebuking, correcting and training in righteousness…" Paul instructs Timothy that God Himself has *breathed* the Bible into life! {II Tim. 3:16, NIV}

Included must be the power of Scripture, displayed in Hebrews, "For the word of God is living and active, sharper than any two-edged sword, piercing to the division of soul and of spirit, of joints and of marrow, and discerning the thoughts and intentions of the heart." Yes, the Word of God is alive, active, and working in all realms, physical, spiritual and intellectual. {Heb. 4:12, ESV}

Capping this perspective, God Himself speaks, "…so is my word that goes out from my mouth: It will not return to me empty but will accomplish what I desire and achieve the purpose for which I sent it." {Is. 55:11, NIV}

God Himself will accomplish His Word! It is our undeserved honor to be His instruments. Thus, armed with the divine assurance of His Word directing us, we continue with great confidence!

Believers have the recorded testimony of Enoch being taken by God, followed by numerous prophecies of the Lord coming back to earth in the books of the Torah or Pentateuch, and throughout the Tanakh, including the Historical books, the Wisdom Literature, and the Major and Minor Prophets.

Then follows accordingly, the testimonies of Jesus during His ministry. The Gospel writings were not published until the mid-first century, roughly a.d. 55-65. Thus, captivatingly, the believing student of the Bible is entranced as scholarship turns the seeker back in time. One discovers the recording of proclamations, plus existing remnants, scrolls, and epistles foretelling the Lord's return. The earliest documented New Testament confirmation of the Rapture is reflected in the a.d. 45-50 epistle of the Apostle James.

Obviously, each epistle and book in the New Testament, including I & II Thessalonians, affords instruction on the Christian life. It is inherently important, therefore, to continue to stress that this work focuses specifically and primarily on the singular, major theme recorded throughout New Testament scripture dealing with the *imminent*, any moment, aspect of the 'snatching away in ecstasy' by Jesus of His Bride.

Our conclusion must be acknowledged that the prophecy of Jesus' 'catching away' His Bride was included with the earliest primary teachings emphasized to the Body. We can thus be assured this doctrine, our 'rapiemur', popularly proclaimed today as the 'Rapture', the word derived from Jerome's 4th-5th century Latin Vulgate translation, is a foundational truth of prophecy.

James

Initial blush to the direct, written reference of the imminent Rapture in this study thus goes to the epistle of James, scrolled by Jesus' half-brother, the son of Joseph and Mary, who eventually was installed as the first pastor of the Jerusalem congregation.

A marvelously deep yet concise work, the book of James' intensity may well be marked by this apostle's conversion to faith, post-Resurrection, in his half-brother also being his Messiah. This would also have exponentially enhanced the reality and nearness of Jesus' any-moment calling out of the Body.

Oblique notation is made of the transitory Christian life in Chapter Four, verses 14-15, "Whereas ye know not what shall be on the morrow. For what is your life? It is even a vapour that appeareth for a little time, and then vanisheth away. For that ye ought to say, If the Lord will, we shall live, and do this, or that." {KJV}

James was addressing the practice of men prematurely projecting their business futures. He corrects them by inserting the proper attitude, '...if the Lord will...' Proverbs 27:1 immediately comes to mind, "Boast not thyself of tomorrow, for thou knowest not what a day may bring forth." {KJV}

Yet, moreover, it is within this very admonition that the attitude toward the imminence of the Rapture is displayed. This any-moment understanding is highlighted in 5:9, as James continues his pastoring, when he supports another necessary Christian response by emphasizing, "The Judge is standing at the door!" {NIV}

How close did James survey Jesus' return for His bride? James said of Jesus, "The Judge *is* standing at the door!"

So, what should our spiritual temperature be with Jesus standing at the door? James has just stated in the previous verses.

> "*⁷Be patient therefore, brethren, unto the coming of the Lord. Behold, the husbandman waiteth for the precious fruit of the earth, and hath long patience for it, until he receive the early and latter rain. ⁸ Be ye also patient; stablish your hearts: for the coming of the Lord draweth nigh." {James 5:7-8; Au-KJV}*

God is persevering in patience, and so should we. Not idle, but focused fellowshipping, and growing and going with and for our Lord.

This was the posture of the believing Church in the early days. This return was even proclaimed by Jesus on the night of His arrest. It was confirmed by the Angel at Jesus' Ascension in Acts 1 and reaffirmed in this first epistle by the Apostle James.

Thus, James emphasizes Jesus' Deity, hearkening back to Abraham's question to the Lord concerning the judgment of Sodom:

> *Far be it from you to do such a thing—to kill the righteous with the wicked, treating the righteous and the wicked alike. Far be it from you! Will not the Judge of all the earth do right?" {Gen. 18:25, NIV}*

Note Abraham's plea for clemency, "...Far be it from *you*! Will not the Judge of all the earth do right?" And now James exclaims to his brothers and sisters in the Lord that Jesus, the *Judge*, stands at the door!

For emphasis, James reminds in 5:10-12 of Tanakh prophets who 'have spoken in the name of the Lord' suffering afflictions and patience, and Job's reward for enduring patience.

Galatians

Galatians is considered one of the earliest of Paul's letters. Scholars suggest that Acts 16 thru 18 place the probability of that writing during the same ministry efforts with the Thessalonians, or even possibly before.

Though shorter than most epistles, Galatians provides a clear, succinct reference to the Lord's shout in 1:4, "⁴ who gave himself for our sins, that he might deliver us

from this present evil world, according to the will of God
and our Father:"

Speaking in the present tense to his audience, Paul is
including himself yet again with 'those who are alive and
remain' being caught up when Jesus 'delivers' believers
from this 'present evil world.' Authority for the teaching
of our Blessed Hope is placed in 'the will of God and our
Father.' Comforting assurance to be sure.

Focusing on "… delivers …", we discover the Greek:
exaireoi – ex-ahee-reh'-o …. From Strong's exhaustive:
"…*act; tear out; select; fig.–to release: deliver, pluck out,
rescue …*"

Sound familiar?

I Thessalonians

Within a short time of its founding, Paul deems it necessary to send a pastoral letter to the young church at
Thessalonica, weaving throughout the epistle the promise
of our Blessed Hope. In fact, Paul closes *each* chapter
with a connective referral to the imminent Rapture,
placing each reference in the present tense.

Multiple times Paul, in this early letter, emphasizes
the expectation and anticipation of God's calling out. Per
example, I Thess. 2:19-20:

> "**19** *For what is our hope, or joy, or crown of
> rejoicing? Is it not even you in the presence of our
> Lord Jesus Christ at His coming?* **20** *For you are
> our glory and joy.*"

"Hope", in this verse, translates more soundly as
'anticipation' as it does continuously throughout many

N.T. references to our Blessed Hope. Ongoing study confirms this perspective.

We followers here in the dawning of the ending age are thus assured how we should be rightly practicing and encouraging one another to continue to do the same. If it was close then, how much closer is it this day in which we are reading this?

Paul urged and then commended these young believers to continue their ministering to one another in I Thess. 5:11, "Wherefore comfort yourselves together, and edify one another, even as also ye do." Comforting and strengthening amplifies at the thought of Jesus snatching us out of this world at any moment on a day that MUST be called 'today.' {KJV}

Paul's teaching of the imminence of the Rapture, rightly placed by James as a hedge against wrong-doing, is set in sharp relief here also as a comfort and strengthening for believers. Encouragement is obviously streaming from Paul's close of the previous chapter as he emphatically proclaims our Blessed Hope!

Acts 17:1-9, documents Paul and Silas' stay in Thessalonica, where Paul first taught and proclaimed the Gospel in the synagogue on three Sabbaths. Some listeners believed Paul while others rejected his message.

Unbelieving Jews, becoming greatly agitated by Paul's proclamations, stirred the city into an uproar crying, "These that have turned the world upside down are come hither also..." {Acts17:6, KJV}

It was to the believing Jews and all others in Thessalonica that had received the Gospel that Paul addressed his first letter, "To the church of the Thessalonians..." {I Thess. 1:1, ESV}

And as we have considered, even though the imminence of the Rapture was taught verbally from the days of Jesus' ministry almost two decades before, I & II Thess., written in a.d. 51, are the first detailed, documented records of the teaching. The passage of chapter 1:9-10, immediately confirms the imminent view practiced by the Thessalonians. "For they, themselves, declare concerning us what manner of entry we had to you, and how you turned to God from idols to serve the living and true God, **and to wait for His Son from heaven**…" {NKJV}

These new believers were already schooled in *anticipating* the return of Jesus from heaven. I Thess. 1:3, "**remembering** *without ceasing your work of faith, labor of love, and patience of* **hope** *in our Lord Jesus Christ in the sight of our God and Father,*"

Importantly, Paul concludes this introductory chapter with a clarifying element of the Rapture, "…even Jesus who *delivers us from the wrath to come.*"

Judgment was coming from God, but believers were to be comforted. God's blessed assurance is that He 'delivers' them from this approaching wrath. In fact, note especially Paul's phrasing in the most current translation of the New King James, wherein the promise of deliverance is framed in the present active voice, '…even Jesus who '*delivers*' us from the wrath to come.' See how neatly folded into this passage is Paul's then active, future perfect, imperative proclamation in I Thess. 4:17b, "…shall be caught up together with them…"

If God were suggesting, rather than prophesying, His promise might merely be interpreted as 'possibility thinking.' But that would remove the proclamation from the active voice and more pertinently from the field of Prophecy altogether.

Paul preached in I Cor. 13:12 that in the present reality of his life he only knew in part, but that the day was approaching when he would know even as he was completely known by God. I John 3:2 explains, "Beloved, now we are children of God; and it has not yet been revealed what we shall be, but we know that when He is revealed, we shall be like Him, for we shall see Him as He is." {KJV; NKJV}

This book is not intended as the be-all or end-all of discussion concerning the imminent Rapture. It is merely an effort to encourage believers as Paul intoned in Galatians 6:10, ministering "...especially unto them who are of the household of faith." That we may cultivate consideration of the event as a further addition to multitudes of excellent studies, sermons, books and observations that have gone before. And all of these are standing in accelerating, pulsating relief to our departure which is rushing down upon us!

Even the writer of Heb. 10:25, clearly affirms a generation that would experience firsthand the Rapture prior to the beginning of the Tribulation, "...not forsaking the assembling of ourselves together, as is the manner of some, but exhorting one another, and so much the more as you see the Day approaching." {NKJV}

Note once more the phrasing in the active voice, present tense of this passage. The writer is affirming the necessity of continuing present exhortations in view of the approaching 'shout' of the Lord. Starkly, the writer is addressing a generation that will in fact '...see the Day approaching.' More of this enticing passage as God permits. Suffice it to say we futurists believe we are that generation, and we are seeing the Day approach!

Hebrews, which we shall examine in order, thus agrees with the imminent aspect recorded in I Thess. 1:10 – "...and to wait for His Son from Heaven, whom He raised from the dead, even Jesus who *delivers* us from the wrath to come." 'Delivers' in the NKJV, the KJV translates as 'delivered,' offering a completed act, for the Greek word which Strong's concordance defines as '...to rush or draw (for oneself,) i.e., to rescue. Thus, it can be read either '...who snatches us from the wrath to come,' or '...who has snatched...'

As with all prophecy, God's proffered eternal viewpoint for our age is that the 'snatch' is already completed! "Jesus Christ the same yesterday, and today, and forever." {Heb. 13:8}

It is my belief that Paul also wrote Hebrews. To reaffirm, yes, I am also in the camp which contends the Apostle Paul wrote Hebrews. The reasons are these: Because He was a Hebrew of the Hebrews. He was a leading teacher of Israel, many suggesting he was in line to be elevated to the seat of Gamaliel (Acts 22:3), should that greatly esteemed teacher retire or die. All of this prior to his Damascus road salvation experience.

Paul even elaborates in his personal, verbal resume' of Gal. 1:14, as he is forced to defend his apostleship, "And I advanced in Judaism beyond many of my contemporaries, in my own nation, being more exceedingly zealous for the traditions of my fathers." {NKJV}

This is only one of many declarations in Paul's ministry pointedly proclaiming his Divine unction, as described by the Apostle John. "But you have an anointing from the Holy One, and all of you know the truth...As for you, the anointing you received from him remains in you, and you do not need anyone to teach you. But as his anointing teaches you about all things and as that anointing is real, not counterfeit—just as it has taught you, remain in him." {I John 2:20 & 27, NIV}

Paul was in the era in which multiplied thousands witnessed themselves or received eye-witness accounts that Jesus was crucified, died, buried, and resurrected on the third day. He held the cloaks of those that stoned Stephen in Acts 7. Paul testified of the hundreds upon hundreds that personally saw Jesus alive following His resurrection from the grave, including the crowd mentioned in I Cor. 15:6, "...After that He {Jesus} was seen by over five hundred brethren *AT ONCE* {author's emphasis}." {KJV}

As to the lack of self-identification which Paul normally used to introduce many of his epistles, like in Galatians per example, signing his name to the Hebrews letter would have sounded the death knell for its reception to his beloved though estranged Israel. This omission could easily be attributed to the virulent animosity against Paul held by so many of the Jewish religious leaders of his day.

Again, Paul continues to press the coming of the Lord for those who are waiting for Him in I Thess. 2:19, "For what is our hope, or joy, or crown of rejoicing? Is it not even you in the presence of our Lord Jesus Christ at His coming?" Here Paul describes the Thessalonian believers as his '*anticipation*' and crown of rejoicing, which they shall become in the presence of our Lord Jesus Christ at His appearing! {NKJV}

When Paul points to 'Jesus Christ at His coming!' is Paul speaking of the Rapture or Jesus' Return to earth? Again, in the context of this letter, written to those who are anticipating 'His Son' 'who delivers us from the wrath to come,' Paul can only be speaking of the pre-Tribulation Rapture since, although the 'wrath' must necessarily fall *before* Jesus returns to the earth, Paul reaffirms in this letter that believers are not 'appointed unto wrath.'

Paul then opens chapter four pleading for purity. Why interject this teaching in the letter? Jesus said His return for His Bride, (see also Luke 17:26-27), would be as in the days of Noah, in which '...the wickedness of man was great on the earth, and that every intent of the thoughts of his heart was only evil continually.' Thus, the anticipation of His Shout answers the demand for purity necessary to ensure worthiness at the trumpet of God and the instantaneous snatching away! {KJV; Gen. 6:5, NKJV}

To truly grasp the evilness of the days of Noah one may read Romans 1, a perfect mirror of today's mores. The ramifications of such perverted practices shall herein remain unplumbed to avoid digressions into those shameful, uninhibited debaucheries. Suffice the discussion to reiterate Jesus' warning that the end times would be like the days of Noah. Let the reader of this chronicled sin, here in this present day, beware.

Paul continues instructing believers to 'love one another' and increase that love 'more and more.' Also, believers are to 'aspire to lead a quiet life,' to 'mind' our own business, to 'work' with our hands, in order to 'walk properly toward those who are outside' the faith, and that we may 'lack nothing.'

Additionally, one is drawn to this call of a quiet life by Enoch's three-century plus walk with God. As others about Him increased their pace of activity, not unlike the practice in living today, Enoch cultivated that meditative, contemplation in step with God's leading. Assuredly there were multiple opportunities for Enoch to be still and know his God.

And we must remember that our Lord Jesus proclaimed, "By this shall all know that ye are disciples of mine, *if ye have love amongst yourselves*." Which dovetails into, "Can two walk together, except they are agreed?" {John 13:35, Darby Bible Translation; Amos 3:3, Webster's Bible Translation}

Finally, beginning in 4:13, Paul addresses eternal life for the believer, beginning with those who die. Paul asserts his teaching that believers not be 'ignorant' about 'those who have fallen asleep.' That is, those who have died. Paul wants the mourners not to 'sorrow as others who have no hope.'

Dr. Gary Frazier points out in his book on the Rapture, "It Could Happen Tomorrow," that most, if not all, preachers strive to avoid mentioning 'those who have no hope,' at funerals. At a funeral everyone wants to believe the person that has just died has gone on to a better place. But here Paul emphasizes, "...those who have no hope." Jesus said anyone who does not believe in Him '...is condemned already...' even *before* they die!

> *"18 He that believeth on him is not condemned: but he that believeth not is condemned already, because he hath not believed in the name of the only begotten Son of God." {John 3:18, Au-KJV}*

Thus, the teaching of the Rapture is an encouragement especially at funerals of those who have lived their lives believing in Jesus.

We accept the credence and surety of the Rapture teaching because in verse 14 Paul proclaims all who believe in the death and resurrection of Jesus can be comforted that Jesus will bring with Him those who 'sleep' in Jesus.

Sticklers will quickly quote correctly that phrase from Verse 14, "…God will bring with Him those who sleep in Jesus." They may be reminded of Jesus' discourse on His Father in John 8, concluding in the Lord's proclamation, "…I am he…" {John 8:28}

Paul next compounds the integrity of this teaching by insisting it is "…the Word of the Lord." Paul is not making this up himself. God has revealed this mystery to Paul! All believers, dead and alive, will be 'snatched up and away', the dead in Christ having been in that moment resurrected for the event. {I Thess. 4:15, NKJV}

Paul assures that Jesus Himself will come down out of heaven with a shout, with the voice of an Archangel, and with the trumpet of God sounding. The dead in Christ shall be the first to be changed, in a moment, in the twinkling of an eye, as they are snatched up in ecstasy to be with Jesus.

All we who remain shall instantaneously be caught up with them, as we also are ecstatically changed from mortal to immortal, ever to be with Jesus!

Chapter five clarifies the timing of the Rapture, as Paul describes the beginning of the Tribulation. He notes that at the very time people begin to say there is peace and safety, sudden destruction shall come upon them and not one will escape. Paul picks up on Jesus' teaching concerning the 'thief' when he notes believers will not be overtaken as with a 'thief' because believers walk in the light as sons of the Light, Jesus.

Verse six reveals two practices Paul instructs believers to follow. Watch, and be sober. He then equates sleeping and drunkenness with the night or darkness. Christians are of the light and not the dark. Here, Paul is emphasizing spiritual realities. One can be standing in broad daylight and be completely immersed in the darkness of sin. Paul encourages believers to cultivate activities that exemplify the Gospel. Beginning with the most obvious, Paul warns against laziness and drunkenness. Jesus also warned in Luke 21:34, "...take heed to yourselves, lest your hearts be weighed down with carousing, drunkenness, and cares of this life, and that Day come on you unexpectedly." Thieves break in unannounced. {NKJV}

Paul speaks of sobriety, affirming the attribute of self-control. Walking in the light, even if we are on the graveyard shift, we should put on the armor of God, Eph. 6:10-18. We are in a spiritual war zone. And we should have 'love' which never fails. I Cor. 13 will humble anyone who thinks they have perfected the love of God.

Again, in verse nine, Paul emphasizes "For God did not appoint us to wrath, but to obtain salvation through our Lord Jesus Christ, ..." {I Thess. 5:9, NKJV}

He declares that dead or alive we believers will be with Jesus, and to continue to comfort each other with these encouraging and strengthening words.

Paul closes I Thess. with exhortations in support of maintaining a watchful vigil for the coming of the Lord. He emphasizes recognizing and esteeming highly those leaders laboring among the local congregations for their service. He underlines peace among the brethren. Warn the unruly. Comfort the fearful. Strengthen the weak. Be patient with everyone.

Instructively, Paul's final charge 'by the Lord' is that this letter of I Thess. be read to *all the brethren*.

"²⁷ I charge you by the Lord that this epistle be read unto all the holy brethren." {I Thess. 5:27, NKJV}

Chapter Eight

The Departure

---

a.d. 51–II Thessalonians

The Gospels and New Testament letters were not all written chronologically or consecutively, as were the epistles to the Corinthians. But I & II Thessalonians have been dated, by many scholars, at least in the same year, 51 a.d.

Dr. James M. Latimer writes in his succinct summation of II Thessalonians,

> *"After preaching his famous Mars Hill sermon, Paul left Athens and went to Corinth. It was there that Silas and Timothy rejoined him, and it was also from there that Paul wrote 1 and 2 Thessalonians, only a few months apart. Most scholars believe that the year was about A.D. 51." {The Christian Life Bible, page 1214.}*

So only a few months had elapsed from the Thessalonian church receiving their first letter when

Paul was moved by the Holy Spirit to send a second. {II Tim. 3:16}

In staying with the intent of this work, we shall only delve into the points Paul imparts relating specifically to the catching away of the Bride of Jesus in this brief, three-chapter epistle. And continuing to focus on the imminence of the Rapture, we shall especially consider Chapter Two, in which Paul delineates specific major end time events as well.

But first, having opened this second letter with his greetings to the Thessalonian congregation, Paul commends them, "…so that we ourselves boast of you among the churches of God for your patience and faith in all your persecutions and tribulations that you endure…" {II Thess. 1:4, NKJV}

> "*7 and to you who are troubled rest with us, when the Lord Jesus shall be revealed from heaven with his mighty angels, 8 in flaming fire taking vengeance on them that know not God, and that obey not the gospel of our Lord Jesus Christ: 9 who shall be punished with everlasting destruction from the presence of the Lord, and from the glory of his power; 10 when he shall come to be glorified in his saints, and to be admired in all them that believe (because our testimony among you was believed) in that day.*"{II Thess. 1:7-10, Au-KJV}

Note Paul has just finished affirming their sufferings make them 'worthy', vs. 5, of the kingdom of God, reminding of Luke 21:36, encouraging the 'troubled' to rest in Jesus until we are revealed with Him upon His return, Rev. 19. Emphasizing that 'rest' shall continue as we return with Jesus 'in flaming fire taking vengeance on them who know not God.' Paul also emphasizes their comfort is enabled by their faith!

Present-day believers may also be greatly comforted to understand that Jesus' admonition that those who follow Him shall in this life have tribulation is by Paul's witness here, manifested in the lives of the believers of Thessalonica. This evidence of suffering shows righteous judgment begins at the house of God, while counting those who suffer as worthy of His kingdom. One is also immediately reminded of Jesus' command in Luke 21:36 to watch and pray always to be counted 'worthy to escape' the judgments prophesied to fall upon the whole world.

Paul follows with a description of that divine wrath that begins and falls throughout the Tribulation. He finishes by describing additional wrath Jesus shall deliver upon His return to earth.

Specifically, concerning the Rapture, Paul embarks on chapter two referencing, "...our gathering together unto Him."

Significantly, Paul highlights in 2:1 the placement of the Rapture as first in the sequence of steps leading to Jesus' returning to earth. "Now, brethren, concerning *the coming of our Lord Jesus Christ and our gathering together to Him...*" Thus, within the context of His coming is placed first and foremost, our gathering unto Him. {NKJV}

Chapter 2:2-3 comforts all believers that the day of the Lord, which begins at the revealing of the Anti-Christ, is not at hand. The King James reads thus: "That ye be not soon shaken in mind, or be troubled, neither by spirit, nor by word, nor by letter as from us, as that *the*

day of Christ is at hand. Let no man deceive you by any means: for *that day shall not come*, except there comes a falling away first, and that man of sin be revealed, the son of perdition…"

Though some scholars teach the 'day of Christ' as given in 2:2, of the KJV, would it not then refer to the Rapture? Many scholars agree the phrase is more accurately translated 'Day of the Lord.'

Significance is appointed to this difference in phrasing because were the 'Day of Christ' the accepted translation, this would put the Rapture after the appearance of the Anti-Christ. Therefore, further scholarship has deduced the correct phrasing should be 'Day of the Lord' which aligns the end time elements with the pre-Tribulation Rapture scenario. If the 'Day of Christ' phrasing is left in place it does violence to the entire end time prophecy outline.

Strikingly, parenthetically, the nexus of His imminent Shout is also destroyed by placing that event within a time-frame, additionally putting much of Scripture's accuracy in question.

This accepted translation of 'Day of the Lord' is evidenced in numerous Bible versions such as the NIV, ESV and NASB for examples. However, James and Peter both stress Jesus is at the door, revealing 'imminence.'

Paul is examining the earthly return of Jesus in this passage, elaborating the prophecy confirmed by John four decades later in Revelation. That period will culminate in the Lord's stepping onto the Mount of Olives following the seven-year Tribulation. His purpose is to differentiate the Day of the Lord from the Rapture, which begins prior to the igniting of the Tribulation.

Paul begins here establishing the unquestioned gathering together of believers to Jesus. He is reaffirming his I Thess. 4 declaration of verses 16-17 in which the Messiah snatches those dead in Christ from their graves first, instantaneously followed by those alive, to be 'caught up' or 'gathered' in the air, ever to be with the Lord!

It is this phrase, 'caught up' from which the word 'rapture', referring to the focus of the Blessed Hope, emanates. As we have already learned, Scripture has revealed references, inferences, allusions, etc., to the doctrine of the 'Rapture.' But of all Scripture connected to this teaching, specifically or otherwise, the phrase 'caught up' reveals the essence of the prophecy that can upend almost any theological discussion concerning the end times.

Caught up: (Rapiemur):

From Perseus Digital Library, Latin Word Study Tool: to seize and carry off, snatch, tear, pluck, drag, hurry away {http://www.perseus.tufts.edu/hopper/morph? =rapiemur&la=la&can=Rapiemur & prior=simul}

Having opened chapter two of Letter II with his declaration of Jesus coming to the sky above the earth to collect His Bride, Paul continues chapter two immediately requesting calm from his disciples, vs. 2, "not to become easily unsettled or alarmed by the teaching allegedly from us—whether by a prophecy or by word of mouth or by letter—asserting that the day of the Lord has already come." Total negation of this prophecy is now growing in popularity today. {NIV}

Heretics had entered into the Thessalonian congregation by letter and presence, teaching the Tribulation, the beginning of the Day of the Lord, had already begun, and believers in Jesus still present had therefore missed the Rapture. So, Paul begins by leading the sheep to still waters, the second duty of a good shepherd.

Leading futurists maintain verse three of this chapter enunciates the order of end time events placing the Rapture first followed by the Tribulation. Daniel substantiates that verse 3 reveals this order, prophesying the Anti-Christ will sign a seven-year covenant with Israel, a fact that brackets the Tribulation with a specific beginning and a timed duration of seven years.

"He will confirm a covenant with many for one 'seven.' In the middle of the 'seven' he will put an end to sacrifice and offering. And at the temple he will set up an abomination that causes desolation, until the end that is decreed is poured out on him." *{Dan. 9:27, NIV}*

Paul states in verse 3, "Let no one deceive you by any means, for that Day will not come unless the falling away comes first, and the man of sin is revealed, the son of perdition." Again, Paul's emphasis on the order is because interlopers had garnered the attention of the Thessalonians, creating unease, deceiving them into believing they had already entered the Tribulation. Paul elaborates on the Rapture sequence detailed in I Thess. 4:13-18, adding new elements to flesh out the prophecy. {NKJV}

Here within the phrase '...that Day...' a clarification is needed. 'Day' actually covers the working out of the end time's scenario which begins following the Rapture. A brief overview reveals the outline of the Day as follows:

Those periods include the Tribulation, next the Return of Jesus to the earth, the separation of the sheep from the goats, the 1,000-year reign, the Great White Throne Judgment and second death, culminating in the beginning of eternity for all, condemned and saved, each in their assigned eternal estates.

It cannot be too strongly emphasized that following the close of 'the Day' eternal Heaven or eternal Hell begins, depending on one's destination. Each of these movements of God has received their own individual studies and continue to be refined as we approach the next major event on God's calendar, the Rapture. Certainly, each deserves continuing consideration. As tempting as the chase is, to go any further would be to digress from the focus of this work which is the *imminence* of the Rapture.

Paul tells the Thessalonians the progression of events begins with the 'apostasia' which more modern translations render as 'a falling away' or a 'leaving of one's faith, belief or religious practice.' Thus, many interpretations have for years taught there is going to come a mass leaving of the Christian faith which takes place before the appearance of the anti-Christ.

This 'falling away' is corroborated by a warning in Heb. 3:12, the passage emphasizing the danger of forsaking fellowship. The falling comes from being led away by deceivers as indicated from the original Greek: *apostēnai — to lead away, to depart from.* A common interpretation of the falling away referenced in II Thess. 2:3 comes from the Greek: Apostasia – defection, revolt. This leads to the understanding that the Anti-Christ will not be revealed until there comes a widespread defection from the faith by believers.

However, there is an earlier usage of the original Greek, *apostasia*, which renders the translation as describing an actual physical leaving as opposed to a spiritual withdrawal.

To prove this point, one only need delve into the original meaning of the Greek word used in II Thessalonians 2:3:

From "A Greek-English Lexicon compiled by Henry Geo. Liddell & Robert Scott, per example, the inquirer discovers 'apostasia' can be interpreted as a '...defection, revolt, rebellion against God...' And this is the accepted interpretation by the majority of professing Christians throughout Christendom today. However, Liddell & Scott note a secondary meaning: 'departure, disappearance.' This definition alludes to the primary meaning of the word as employed at the time of Paul.

In fact, an outstandingly definitive work focusing on the imminence of the Rapture as related to end time events is "The Departure: God's Next Catastrophic Intervention into Earth's History." This treatise, helmed by General Editor and contributing author Terry James, comprises a number of prominent Christian scholars who prefer this earlier definition of 'departure' over the more popular interpretation.

Derived from the Greek 'apostasia' of II Thessalonians 2:3, in his introduction, entitled 'One Giant Leap,' James concurs, "The 'falling away' term of this passage in the King James Version is taken from the Greek noun apostasia.

Extensive studies in the Scriptures confirm for the authors of this book that this word in almost every case means a 'departure from'—a physical departure." {*Pg22, para. 3, The Departure: God's Next Catastrophic Intervention into Earth's History; Defender Publishing Group, Crane, Missouri 65633*}

So rather than this prophecy relating to a 'falling away from the faith of the Bible,' it is simply pointing out that before the Tribulation, and '...that Day...', begins, the Blessed Hope, the Rapture, the Great Ecstatic Snatch will occur.

This view is attested to by all 17 primary contributors to that work, plus all of the additional contributing writers submitting to 'The Departure' position. Contributor Paul Lee Tan affirms, for example: *"The best translation of the word (apostasia) is 'to depart'. The apostle Paul refers here to a definite event which he calls 'the departure' and which will occur just before the start of the Tribulation. This is the Rapture of the church."* {*From: 'The Departure: God's next catastrophic intervention into Earth's history," pg. 370, para. 2 quoting: Paul Lee Tan, The Interpretation of Prophecy, (Winona Lake, IN: Assurance Publishers, 1974) pg. 341.*}

Allusion is made to the Rapture in verses 7-8 of chapter Two. "For the mystery of lawlessness is already at work; only He who now restrains will do so until He is *taken out of the way.* And then the lawless one will be revealed..."

This action of the Holy Spirit being 'taken out of the way' is often noted by futurists pointing to the 'catching away' of believers. Being indwelt by the Holy Spirit, it takes no imagination to connect the Bride's elopement with the Holy Spirit relinquishing His protective role on earth.

God restrains the evil in the world, not allowing sin to grow beyond designated boundaries, Rom. 1:18-32, through the power of the Holy Spirit.

> *Rom. 1:26, "Because of this, God gave them over to shameful lusts. Even their women exchanged natural sexual relations for unnatural ones." {NIV}*

From Paul's Rom. 1:26 declaration, it is readily understood the restraining of the Holy Spirit is taken out of the way. The earth dwellers shall again be given free rule in their lustful passions, as in the days of Noah, men for men and women for women, among other sinful pursuits per example. All vestiges of morality shall vanish from the *'earth dwellers.'* {See Dr. T. Ice's dissertation on the 'earth dwellers'. {pre-trib.org}

After the Holy Spirit steps out of the way, escorting the Bride of Messiah to her Groom, the lawless one, the Anti-Christ, will be revealed.

Chapter Nine

Waiting for Jesus

---

a.d. 59–I Corinthians

Majority dating ascribes Paul to have written I Corinthians in 59 a.d. The Synoptic Gospels, Matthew, Mark, and Luke are also dated as being scribed in this decade, even possibly to this year of Paul's first surviving letter to the church of God in Corinth.

This dating would mean the Book of James, both Thessalonian epistles, Galatians, possibly the Gospels, and perhaps Romans had already been in circulation for nearly a decade at least, establishing a familiarity with the teaching of the Rapture amongst many congregations planted throughout the Middle East. At the very least an introduction to the prophecy had been made to most.

Combined, that would make I Corinthians the ninth or tenth recognized source documenting the imminent Rapture during the first generation of believers.

This initial Corinthian letter is replete with passages linked one way and another to our Blessed Hope. I Corinthians 1:7 introduces the reader to the perspective

125

of the Corinthian believers regarding the promise of our ecstatic snatching away.

"*...eagerly waiting for the revelation of our Lord Jesus Christ.*" Roughly eight years have passed since Paul's letters to the Thessalonians were received. Yet, Paul commends the Corinthians by way of introduction to their faithfulness to '*...be...*' (*Present* tense) '**eagerly waiting**' for the revelation of our Lord Jesus. There is evidently then, though nearly a decade has passed, no loss of interest concerning the promise of an 'any moment' calling out by the Lord. {NKJV}

Paul had commended the Thessalonians for waiting for the '*...one true God...*', and here nearly a decade later, Paul is congratulating Corinthian believers for steadfastly, '*eagerly*' waiting for the Lord. 'Eagerly' waiting then is the commended posture of believers and congregations. And how much more should we in this present hour be refreshing that anticipation for His Shout?

To emphasize the importance of the Corinthian attention to the imminence of the Rapture, Paul declares in I Cor. 7:29-31:

> "*But this I say, brethren, the time is short, so that from now on even those who have wives should be as though they had none, those who weep as though they did not weep, those who rejoice as though they did not rejoice, those who buy as though they did not possess, and those who use this world as not misusing it. For the form of this world is passing away.*" {NKJV}

How short was Paul saying the time had become? Here in verse 29 is where Paul first distinguishes this

instruction as a specific demarcation, '...from now on...'
Believers were to immediately, and forthwith daily,
renew their minds from this point on, viewing their walk
'from this moment forward'.

How can one capture this perspective? God had instituted marriage immediately following the creation of Eve,
declaring, "Therefore a man shall leave his father and
mother and be joined to his wife, and they shall become
one flesh." Now Paul was asserting a new dynamic into
marital bliss. Those in wedlock were to 'be as though'
they were not. {Gen. 2:24, NKJV}

Paul was not promoting either abstinence or promis-
cuity. Earlier, in this chapter, 7:5, Paul intones, "Do not
deprive one another except with consent for a time, that
you may give yourselves to fasting and prayer; and come
together again so that Satan does not tempt you because
of your lack of self-control." Here, Paul was affirming
the proper conduct of a married couple to engage reg-
ularly in sexual intercourse, with consent, individually
taking time for fasting and prayer, coming together again
following that devotion to God. {ESV}

Paul is instructing the husband and wife to practice consistent, regular marital bliss. This practice is a
guard against Satan tempting you because of your lack
of self-control. Moreover, couples are advised to avoid
being deprived of physical contact longer than is healthy
for the relationship of both the husband and the wife.

Then, in 7:29, Paul is saying that the time is short, so
couples must *from now on* react as those who are unmarried. Paul clarifies, in verse 32, "I would like you to be free
from concern. An unmarried man is concerned about the
Lord's affairs—how he can please the Lord." This does
not negate the marriage obligations; couples are only to

withhold their favors 'for a time' and then come together again. Their outward walk should be as singles.

Paul, in speaking of being as if they are not married, merely addresses husbands and wives to the primary role of waiting, watching and witnessing as they daily antici- pate the Lord's Trump!

Similarly, the singles are to act as married to be faithful to their Lord. Paul even stresses in verse 9, "But if they cannot exercise self-control, they should marry. For it is better to marry than to burn with passion." And also, from I Cor. "...all things decently and in order." {I Cor. 14:40; ESV}

Paul underlines this perspective by continuing with other normal states of human response. To those 'who weep', finds some in the throes of sorrow. Some are at this moment rejoicing. Others are involved in commerce. Still more are using this world. To each Paul is advising 'temperance,' a word badly distorted in this present age. 'Temperance' is not abstinence. Temperance is modera- tion. Once again, Paul turns to 'decency and order,'

Philippians 4:5 not only endorses this instruction, it confirms once again how closely our walk is aligned to the imminent Rapture. "Let your moderation be known unto all men. The Lord *is* at hand." What can appear to be actions of shallowness or weak commitment can in fact be responses to cultivating that preparation for the Lord's any moment calling out! {KJV}

And from where does one receive such holy restraint? I John 3:3, "And everyone who has this hope in Him purifies himself, just as He is pure." More on this later, the Lord willing! {NKJV}

Thus, our main focus in this chapter is on the reality that the proper perspective concerning the Rapture is the recognition that 'the time is short.' Spiritually speaking, it always has been temporal, but now the end is in sight.

<u>*God's Especial Promise to Israel*</u>
{To carry them through the Tribulation}

Hos. 6:1-3, NIV-UK, prophesies the Lord's return to earth will be accomplished on the third day:

> *"'Come, let us return to the Lord.*
> *He has torn us to pieces*
> *but he will heal us;*
> *he has injured us*
> *but he will bind up our wounds.*
> *² After two days he will revive us;*
> *on the third day he will restore us,*
> *that we may live in his presence.*
> *³ Let us acknowledge the Lord;*
> *let us press on to acknowledge him.*
> *As surely as the sun rises,*
> *he will appear;*
> *he will come to us like the winter rains,*
> *like the spring rains that water the earth."*

Knowing that God Himself proclaimed, "⁸ But, beloved, be not ignorant of this one thing, that one day is with the Lord as a thousand years, and a thousand years as one day." {II Peter 3:8}

We can now retrospectively see that Hosea was speaking of an event two thousand years into the future.

From that point in fact, one can easily ascertain we are now at the beginning of the third thousand years

129

from Jesus' departure making this the morning of the third day!

Yet how can we be sure? And why, on all of God's green earth, would Israel return to praying Jesus' prophesied prayer of Israel's in the last days, "… baruch haba b'shem Adonai?"

Following the events prophesied clarifies the interpretation. Chapter divisions being a relatively new inclusion, we return to the verses ending the previous chapter, Hos. 5:14-15, NIV-UK:

> *"For I will be like a lion to Ephraim,*
> *like a great lion to Judah.*
> *"I will tear them to pieces and go away;*
> *I will carry them off, with no one to rescue them.*
> *"15 Then I will return to my lair*
> *until they have borne their guilt*
> *and seek my face –*
> *in their misery*
> *they will earnestly seek me."*

Here we see the foreshadowing of several prophecies. Verse 14 describes the scattering of Israel to the four winds in 70 a.d. Verse 15 reveals Jesus' ascension and purpose. Zech. 12:10 describes Israel's repentance at their rejection of Jesus which concludes verse 15, neatly dovetailing into 6:1.

And the Lord's return on the third day will be heralded by Israel's seeking His face. Jesus prophesied this seeking in Matt. 23:39, "For I tell you, you will not see me again until you say, *"Baruch haba b'Shem Adonai."* 'Blessed is he who comes in the name of the Lord.'" {NIV}

Knowing Jesus shall return to earth at the end of the seven-year Tribulation as revealed in Rev. 19, and understanding Jesus promised an escape from the trials to fall upon the earth in Luke 21:36, leads us back to the imminent Rapture and His calling out.

Jesus' approaching call is verified in the posture of the Corinthian church already lauded by Paul in I Cor. 1:7, as they *'eagerly'* await His revelation! {BSB}

As to the crown of righteousness Paul promises in II Timothy 4:8 to all those who love His appearing, here in I Cor. 9:26 the Apostle explains, in his race for the crown, he runs thus: not with uncertainty. "Thus, I fight not as one who beats the air." Paul is poised and focused. {NKJV}

As Paul reminds the Thessalonians the prophecy of the imminent Rapture is supported by the very teaching of the Crucifixion. He underscore's that reality here in I Cor. 11:26 as he gives instruction on the Lord's Supper:

"For as often as you eat this bread and drink the cup, you proclaim the Lord's death until he comes." {ESV}

So, even as we believers commemorate the Lord's death we are encouraged to be simultaneously looking forward to His calling out. Parenthetically, the importance of proclaiming the Lord's death may seem to some as unnecessary, and even redundant. Yet, proclamations that Jesus was never crucified, and *that He never died,* such as taught in Islam's Koran, reveal the absolute necessity of persevering in broadcasting the Gospel, I Cor. 15:1-4. *{Au-KJV)}*

> *"1Moreover, brethren, I declare unto you the gospel which I preached unto you, which also ye have received, and wherein ye stand; ² by which also ye are saved, if ye keep in memory what I preached unto you, unless ye have believed in vain. ³ For I delivered unto you first of all that which I also received, how that Christ died for our sins according to the scriptures; ⁴ and that he was buried, and that he rose again the third day according to the scriptures:..." {&, Col. 1:22, 1599 Geneva Bible – GNV}*

Sura (chapter) 4.157-8

That Koranic passage reads at http://quod.lib.umich.edu/k/koran/: "[4.157] *And their saying: Surely we have killed the Messiah, Isa (Jesus) son of Marium (Mary), the apostle of Allah; and they did not kill him nor did they crucify him, but it appeared to them so (like Isa) and most surely those who differ therein are only in a doubt about it; they have no knowledge respecting it, but only follow a conjecture, and they killed him not for sure.*

[4.158] *Nay! Allah took him up to Himself; and Allah is Mighty, Wise.*"

Such a bedrock biographical contradiction conflicting these two major world religions' theological positions, especially concerning the life and death of Jesus, highlights the total incompatibility of these two messages and their sources. Christians also realize another significant reason why celebrating the Lord's Supper is paramount to the preaching of the Gospel.

In I Cor. 15:51-52 Paul unfolds the mystery of the Rapture. Not the secret Rapture, but the hidden truth of the prophecy that is now being revealed. "Listen, I will tell you a mystery: We will not all sleep, but we will all be changed—in a moment, in the blinking (twinkling) of an eye, at the last trumpet. For the trumpet will sound, and the dead will be raised imperishable, and we will be changed." {NET Bible.}

Use of the word 'mystery' in Paul's day and culture meant to reveal something that was hidden rather than the modern understanding of an unknown or secret event.

At the writing of I Corinthians nearly a decade has passed since the inscribing of I and II Thess., and Paul is instructing new believers, while divulging further details of the event, continuing to prepare them, as he did the Thess. congregation, for the 'any moment' imminent Rapture!

We know from Paul's teaching in I Thess. 4:13-18, that he is speaking here of the Rapture. I Cor. 15:53-55 is often applied at Christian funerals of loved ones who have died, attributing these verses to the resurrection to follow at the end of the tribulation, or the raising of the dead at the close of the thousand-year reign.

"Context, context, context," is the favorite refrain of Bible teachers. Exegetical preaching is rightly demanded by scholars. Merriam-Webster defines 'exegesis' as, "…an explanation or critical interpretation of a text." Therefore, this encouragement in context is to the singular appli-cation of the Rapture. We know this because this entire chapter focuses on the reality of the imminent Rapture.

This explains why Paul emphasized immediacy so strongly to Timothy in II Tim. 4:2, "Preach the word; be instant in season, out of season…" Strong's 4493 ren-ders an additional definition for 'twinkling' as, "…in an instant…" Astoundingly, *'twinkling'* is found only once in the entire Bible, in this very passage of verse 52! That by itself underscores God's desire to emphasize the singular mystery of the imminence. Repeatedly, throughout the Gospels Jesus is described employing immediacy, acting instantaneously. And so, shall it be in that hallowed, sanctified moment of the snatching up of His Bride. {KJV}

For Paul notes, "For this corruptible (the dead in Christ) must put on incorruption, and this mortal (we who are alive and remain) must put on immortality. So, when this corruptible has put on incorruption, and this mortal has put on immortality, then shall be brought to pass the saying that is written, Death is swallowed up in victory. 'O Death, where is your sting? O Hades, where is your victory?" {I Cor. 15:53-55, NKJV}

When shall these divine transformations ensue? When the dead in Christ are raised and we who are alive and remain are caught up with them! Thus, the corruptible (the dead) shall put on incorruption, the mortal (temporal) put on immortality fulfilling the reality of death being swallowed up in victory and the sting of death foiled by the intervening, snatching away of the living!

Paul closes this letter in verse 16:22 with the word Christians of the first-generation church employed both in greetings of salutations and farewells. In the Greek 'maranatha,' and in the English, 'O, Lord Come!' { NKJV}

For the 1st century Christians were not simply aimlessly wandering around, waiting for the Lord's return, they were expectantly anticipating His calling out at any moment from their fields of labor!

How often have you heard the exclamation, "Oh, how I wish we were like the first century Christians. How exactly can we be like the early Church?"

This attitude of receiving completely the teaching of the imminent, any moment snatching away by Jesus will assuredly transport such desires toward reality!

Doubtless also, such anticipation will encourage all to keep busy! Who wants to be found not laboring when the Master appears?

Chapter Ten

Eagerly with Perseverance

---

a.d. 57-60–Romans
a.d. 60–II Corinthians
a.d. 60-63–I Peter
a.d. 60-64–II Peter

As early as 57 to 60 a.d. four new epistles appeared on the Christian scene. This would bring the total letters and epistles available to seekers of God at roughly a dozen.

Romans

Dating allows for an a.d. 57 *Romans* publication, while some set the writing as late as a.d. 60.

Romans opens with Paul's focusing on faith in 5:2, focusing on our hope and Glory, Jesus' elopement. "² by whom also we have access by faith into this grace wherein we stand, and rejoice in hope, (anticipation), of the glory of God." {Romans, Au-KJV}

Then Paul powerfully interjects the promised surety of Jesus' deliverance of His Bride at the Shout in 5:9: "⁹

Much more then, being now justified by his blood, we shall be saved from wrath through him." Showcasing the power and purpose of Jesus' shed blood, Paul again reminds believers are not appointed unto God's wrath.

Which brings us to an especially delightful revelation written in the same time period, suggesting again Paul's maturing understanding into the developing history of the Church. In Rom. 8:18-25 we read:

"For I consider that the sufferings of this present time are not worthy to be compared with the glory which shall be revealed in us. For the earnest expectation of the creation eagerly waits for the revealing of the sons of God. For the creation was subjected to futility, not willingly, but because of him who subjected it in hope {anticipation}; because the creation itself also will be delivered from the bondage of corruption into the glorious liberty of the children of God. For we know that the whole creation groans and labors with birth pangs together until now. Not only that, but we also who have the firstfruits of the Spirit, even we ourselves groan within ourselves, eagerly waiting for the adoption, the redemption of our body. For we were saved in this hope, but hope that is seen is not hope; for why does one still hope for what he sees? But if we hope for what we do not see, we eagerly wait for it with perseverance." {NKJV}

In this Romans 8 passage then, Paul ascertains the certainty of eternal security, the completeness of salvation in Jesus, evidenced by the believer walking in the power of the Spirit of God. He adversely emphasizes in the verses leading to the passage we are considering the surety of eternal suffering guaranteed to those who submit to the carnality of this age.

He contrasts this eternal reality against the promised temporal suffering of those who follow Jesus. Hebrews proclaims there is pleasure in sin for a season. Conversely, suffering is only for a season. This obvious balance is seldom made plain in present-day congregations. Yet Paul urges here that this temporary pleasure shall reap eternal damnation.

Thus, in 8:18, Paul reckons the sufferings the believer is blessed to endure from following Jesus in this present age, are not worthy to be compared with the glory *which shall be revealed* in us. Paul is speaking to the joy we shall enter into at the Rapture.

This promise is linked with John's in I John 3:2, "... and it has not yet been revealed what we shall be, but we know that when He is revealed, we shall be like Him..." This joy will not be a culmination but an eternal beginning of delight! And that eternal delight shall *be revealed* at the moment of ecstatic Rapture and exponentially magnify as we gain the presence of our Lord and Savior Jesus Christ, Yeshua Ha Maschiach! {NKJV}

Paul then instructs even creation is groaning with *eager expectation* because it too shall be delivered from the bondage of corruption thrust upon it in the Garden of Eden at the fall of man. And we also, Paul points out, groan with that same *eager anticipation*, even for those of us whose bodies are in the grave that shall be redeemed in resurrection in that moment, that twinkling of an eye, when we all in Christ shall be changed, our corruptible bodies, both dead and alive, putting on incorruption!

Acknowledging the ethereal manifestation of our hope, Paul enjoins us to hope for that which we do not see, that in faith we might please Him who shall come to deliver us! Thus we, "...*eagerly wait for it* <u>with perseverance</u>." KJV//Strong's Exhaustive Concordance – '<u>patience</u>': 'cheerful (or hopeful) endurance, constancy; {Rom. 8:25; God's Word Translation}

Paul clings to this perspective in Rom. 13:11-12 declaring, "...for now is our salvation nearer than when we believed...the day is at hand..." {KJV}

Once again, the Apostle extraordinaire returns to the 'imminence' of this prophecy, agreeing with Peter and James that...*the day is at hand, He is at the Door!*

We grasp the implication when pondering the timing, "...at hand..." In Mark 14:42, Jesus declares, "Rise, let us be going; see, my betrayer is at hand." This is the Lord's response as the mob approaches to arrest Him, led by Judas Iscariot. This is how close the imminent Rapture is described, it is "...at hand." {ESV}

Finally, in summation, Paul plants the stake to which all doctrine is purposed for the believer, closing with 14:10-12, "...we shall *all* stand before the judgment seat of Christ..." Said another way, each believer shall one day stand before the judgment seat of Christ and give an account of all things done in the flesh. And that appearance follows closely the entry of the imminent, any moment, and eternal 'rapiemur' out of our present existence.

II Corinthians

During this same time period, in 60 a.d., Paul writes his second epistle to the Corinthians, a year after the first, referencing the end times and the Rapture. Again, as study continues, we look forward to these writings being more perfectly joined in their sequential order, the perfection of which shall more expertly clarify the depths and wonders of the Word.

In II Cor. 1:13-14 Paul states, "For we are not writing to you anything other than what you read and understand and I hope you will fully understand — just as you did partially understand us — that on the day of our Lord Jesus you will boast of us as we will boast of you." Here Paul spans the scope of the believer's life in Jesus, prefacing his view of the snatching away with his reference looking to the Rapture, "For we write nothing else to you than what you read and understand, and I hope you will understand until the end..." as Peter had done.

{ESV; II Cor. 1:13, NASB}

Paul comforts the Corinthian believers with his reminder he shall be 'our' boast as 'we' in the body of Messiah will be Paul's and His 'crown' in another passage, "...in the day of the Lord Jesus..." Which manifests in the Rapture, to, "...always be with the Lord." This last a reminder of Paul's initial revelation in I Thess. 4:17c, "...and so shall we ever be with the Lord."

In verse 14 of II Cor. 4 Paul connects the theme of I Thess. 4:14, with his affirmation, "...knowing that He who raised up the Lord Jesus will also raise us up with Jesus and will present us with you." Not mere coincidence, Paul here emphasizes, "...and will present us *with* you to himself." {NKJV}

Once again, Paul establishes the reality of I Thess. 4:13-18. First, Paul describes Jesus raising us up Himself, and then completes the description by emphasizing we shall be presented with Paul. This of course blends perfectly with Jesus' encouragement to Peter that a day was coming when Jesus would 'receive' Peter unto Himself.

Also, 2 Cor. 4-14, connects with Jesus' resurrection. Paul describes how Jesus shall 'raise us up.' The immediacy of the Rapture, first revealed in the early 50's of the 1st century in the present tense as 'we who are alive and remain,' now almost a decade later, is presented as a future, more detailed, event in which Paul will be raised from the dead, along with 'you'. Yet, the imminence focused on in I Thess. 4:17 is never revoked. {NKJV; KJV}

In II Cor. 12:2-4 Paul testifies to his own Rapture experience some 14 years prior, which was first noted in this work's *'Blast Off, Chapter Three'*. Consistently, Paul employs the same exact root word in I Thess. 4, rendered most times in English translations as 'caught up.' **Jerome's usage in I Thess. and II Cor. 12 stream from the same Latin root, 'rapio.' II Cor. 12:4: 'raptus,' is past tense, defined as 'rapture, rape, rip-off,' revealing a theft! 'Rapiemur' is future perfect, 'to be snatched with ecstasy.' 12:2, 'raptum', defines as 'spoil, loot, trophy', for God!** This usage glaringly displays the action warning to unbelievers of the event. Paul experienced it unexpectedly and preaches from his experience!

Also, intriguing is that Paul documents this confirming testimony of his own personal Rapture over a decade after the occurrence only when pressured to affirm his apostleship. Yet the experience stood him in excellent stead to instruct the Thessalonians on an unimaginable Blessing in their possession.

I Peter

The Apostle Peter surfaces next as an author of the Good News and by extension the Blessed Hope. Both his epistles are adjudged to have been written closely together. I Peter between a.d. 60-63, roughly nine years following the first delivery of I & II Thess., with II Pet. following between a.d. 60-64.

Peter immediately encourages the reader in his salutation, rejoicing in 1:3, "...to a *living* hope..." accentuating the active voice of declaration heavily emphasizing Christians are not simply 'pie in the sky' dreamers. He cements the reality in verse 4, preaching, "...to an inheritance incorruptible and undefiled and that does not fade away, reserved in heaven for you..." One cannot corrupt that which rests eternally within the very Word of God. {NKJV}

Pursuing an orderly, chronological progression of revelations on the teaching of the imminence of the Rapture, we first consider Peter's audience are those suffering persecution. Many will even give their lives for Jesus. Paul's encouragement, '...And the dead in Christ shall rise first...' is approaching personal reality to many of these believers. Thus, Peter's salutation, '... begotten us again to a *living* hope...' is far beyond mere words. Peter continues in I Peter: 1:5, "...who are kept by the power of God through faith for salvation *ready to be revealed in the last time,*" reinforcing Paul's prophecy of the Rapture. Verse 7 assuring Peter's focus on the Shout, "... at the appearing of Jesus Christ:" { NKJV; Au-KJV}

Enumerating additional references in I Peter, we find 1:13, 21; 3:3-4, 15, 4:12-13.

And, I Peter: 4:7, "But the end of *all* things is at hand, therefore be *serious* and *watchful* in your prayers." Here he, who is also called Cephas, directs the believers to look to the end of *all* things in the last time. Peter's use of 'at hand' demonstrates another perfect example of life swifter than a weaver's shuttle. {NKJV}

Jesus had commanded the disciples to become aware and witness the events that would begin to shape the end times, and that they might strive to be counted 'worthy to escape' all the trials that were going to fall upon the whole world. Peter now alludes to that escape for those who are saved, both dead and alive. And, again, in 5:1, as he speaks of '...the glory that will be revealed.'

Then we who are watching for His appearing are assured of Peter's intentions in verse 4, "...and when the Chief Shepherd appears, you will receive the crown of glory that does not fade away." Paul will describe another crown nearly a decade later as he prepares for his own demise in II Timothy 4:8. These apostles are speaking of different crowns!

II Peter

Peter reminds believers in II Pet. 1:16, "For we have not followed cunningly devised fables, when we made known unto you the power and coming of our Lord Jesus Christ but were eyewitnesses of his majesty." {KJV}

Addressing the return of the Lord in the present tense confirms for the reader Peter's own faith of anticipating the Lord's coming back.

This letter goes on to include warnings and instructions concerning false teachers that will enter in among believers. Specifically addressing the promise of Jesus returning to the earth, Peter reveals in II Pet. 3:3-4, "…knowing this first: that scoffers will come in the last days, walking according to their own lusts, and saying, 'Where is the promise of His coming? For since the fathers fell asleep, all things continue as they were from the beginning of creation.'" {NKJV}

A primary evidence the last days are upon the world will be the increasing ridicule prophetical proclamations will receive as the world approaches the end of this age. Can you hear the echo of laughter yet?

Especially note in this passage the exposure of professing believers in Jesus. These acknowledge Genesis 1, and ironically use the testimony of God creating the world as proof that the proclamation of Jesus returning is therefore false because Jesus has still not come back.

Peter counters these heresies with his own acknowledgment of creation from the Genesis account, and explains the delay of the Lord's return, "The Lord is not slow in keeping his promise, as some understand slowness. Instead he is patient with you, *not wanting anyone to perish*, but everyone to come to repentance." {II Pet. 3:9, NIV}

At which point he reiterates the prophecy of the Day of the Lord, also warning the day will come '…as a thief in the night…' {II Pet., 3:10} This proximity to the Rapture description suggests the revelation of the Anti-Christ and covenant with Israel will follow sooner after the 'great snatch' than some scholars project.

Peter then expands the prophecy by including the passing away of the heavens at the end of the millennium, the elements melting with fervent heat, as "both the earth and the works that are in it will be burned up." {II Peter 3:10, NASB}

Looking to that final end Peter focuses on one's spiritual walk in 3:11-12, asking, "...Therefore...what manner of persons ought you to be in holy conduct and godliness, looking for and hastening the coming of the day of God, because of which the heavens will be dissolved, being on fire, and the elements will melt with fervent heat." {NKJV}

Immediately Peter comforts in 3:13 with the reminder, "Nevertheless we, according to His promise, look for new heavens and a new earth..." Several passages help to fix the timing of these stark end-time prophecies that outline the transition into eternity.

Jesus, of course, spoke of the thief in the night nearly three decades before, in the Gospels, preparing those with ears to hear for the imminent 'Shout' of the Rapture. Peter's metaphorical allusion to the Day of the Lord stealing on the earth as a thief in the night aligns perfectly with Jesus' warning of the suddenness of the Rapture. These declarations couple with Paul's pronouncement in I Thess. 1:10 that Jesus, "...delivers us from the wrath to come..." assuring believers they will be with the Lord forever from the Rapture forward, missing the Tribulation completely. All of this given three millennia before the destruction of the old earth and the appearance of the new that Peter views. {ESV}

Delightfully, Peter includes the imminent Rapture as a mere addendum when he notes, "...looking for and hastening the coming of the day of God."

The 'day of God', refers to the beginning of our eternal state. But, where is the mention of the imminent Rapture in this passage one might ask? It is not even mentioned. Well said.

However, Peter's acknowledgement of the imminent Rapture is inherent in verse 3:14, "Therefore, beloved, since you are waiting for these, *__be diligent to be found by him__* without spot or blemish, and at peace." What need of diligence if the Rapture is far away? Why would diligence be necessarily placed in such high priority? To what purpose is this emphasis for present holiness? How shall we be found? By Him, in a moment, in the twinkling of an eye! {ESV}

Also note, this encouragement is directed specifically to those who believe in the imminent Rapture! Peter declares, "…since you **are** waiting for these…"

Paul instructs believers are not appointed to wrath, speaking of God's wrath to fall in the Tribulation. The seven-year Tribulation begins with Israel signing the Anti-Christ's covenant prior to the Lord's return to earth, Dan. 9:26 with II Thess. 2:3d. Both in turn reflect back on Paul's annunciation that Jesus will be calling His Bride out as disclosed, "…for that Day will not come…" unless the '*apostasia*' or '*departure*' comes first.

Peter's II: 3:12-14 admonitions fold neatly into Paul's Rapture reference. "…waiting for and hastening the coming of the day of God, because of which the heavens will be set on fire and dissolved, and the heavenly bodies will melt as they burn," describes the proper and earnest desiring for the beginning of eternity with God. {ESV}

Peter stitches all of these events neatly together in verse 14 of that passage while again alluding to the imminent Rapture. "So then, dear friends, since you are looking forward to this, *make every effort to have the Lord find you at peace and without spot or fault*." (ISV.)

The Rapture is not the end for Christians but the fulfillment of our beginning with Jesus when we were saved! We are not looking forward to 40 acres of cloud with a rocking chair and a harp.

Spectacular Eternal reality beyond imagination awaits all who trust in Him.

> "⁹ But as it is written:
> "Eye has not seen, nor ear heard,
> Nor have entered into the heart of man
> The things which God has prepared
> for those who love Him."
> {I Cor. 2:9, NKJV)

As a side note, Dr. Jason Lisle, astrophysicist, commendably offers those interested in a leap into the depths of our universe his delightful *"Taking Back Astronomy."** Lisle confirms science recognizes the universe is continuing to expand, while simultaneously emphasizing there are "…innumerable galaxies." One therefore understands even the number of galaxies is in fact unknown in a universe that is also growing! There will be no boredom in Heaven! *(Chapter 1, page 21, *Taking Back Astronomy*, Master Books, New Leaf Publishing, 2006.)

This present life is nothing more than a vapor, a miserable anteroom by comparison to the adjoining entrance of Eternal Glory with God!

> *"¹⁴ whereas ye know not what shall be on the morrow. For what is your life? It is even a vapour, that appeareth for a little time, and then vanisheth away."* {*James 4:14, Au-KJV*}

For all hungering for further glimpses into God's reality for eternity read Lisle's *"Taking Back Astronomy."*

And Peter cautions believers in verse 14 to be mindful of the Lord's imminent calling out since He is at hand, preparing at any moment to snatch His sheep from harm's way. The big fisherman's encouragement is that we be found by Jesus in peace, and without spot or fault. We need to be ready!

Having thus drawn the picture of the any moment return of the Lord for His Bride, may the II Pet. 3:14 calling to holiness be emphasized, "…be diligent to be found by Him in peace, without spot and blameless." Note this NKJV rendition renders the NIV translation of 'make every effort,' to 'be diligent.' The two instructions support and integrate with each other seamlessly.

Thus, Paul's concentrated theme in his Thessalonian letters, highlighting the imminent Rapture is continued through Peter's epistles.

Why should all this effort be made to anticipate the Shout?

Certainly, at least a few more dozen reasons could be listed. The promised Crown, for one? And, meanwhile, without question, the promised comfort and strength bestowed.

In this day and age in which we are living in 2019, John's admonition also fits exquisitely: "³ And everyone who has this hope in Him purifies himself, just as He is pure." {I John 3:3, NKJV}

But firstly, because quite simply, that we might please Him.

Chapter Eleven

His Upward Call

---

a.d. 61-64–Ephesians
a.d. 62–Acts
a.d. 63-64–Philippians
a.d. 63-64–Colossians
a.d. 64–Hebrews
a.d. 64—I Timothy

Ephesians

Paul's writing of Ephesians is placed by historians at between a.d. 61-64.

Ephesians is viewed by many Bible scholars and Christians as 'the Alps of the New Testament'. Here, Paul crystallizes God's perception of time in the singularity of this event called the Rapture. "That in the dispensation of the fullness of the times He might gather together in one all things in Christ, both which are in heaven and which are on earth—in Him." {1:10, NKJV}

Paul reflects on God's sovereignty, noting that all of time submits to Him 'with whom we have to do.' And in the perfect moment He shall 'gather' into one body all who are in Messiah, those gone before with all who yet are alive and remain in this world unto Himself. {Heb. 4:13, NASB}

It may again be emphasized that Paul's recognition of God's sovereignty did not inhibit his evangelical outreach. "To the weak became I as weak, that I might gain the weak: I am made all things to all men that I might by all means save some." {I Cor. 9:22, KJV}

Saved unto? Verses 1:9-14, engrave the full measure of that which emanates in His Shout. That 'mystery which has been 'revealed' to us 'predestined' according to 'His good pleasure', 'after His own will', 'in the fullness of times' 'He might gather unto Himself' all in Christ, 'both' in heaven and on earth, that 'we should be to the praise of His Glory', 'in whom ye trusted' 'after that ye heard the truth' 'sealed with that Holy Spirit of promise', the 'earnest of our inheritance' 'unto the redemption of the purchased possession' ...."

In Eph. 4:30, Paul cautions, "And do not grieve the Holy Spirit of God, by whom you were sealed for the day of redemption." As he warns elsewhere, we must strive to meet the Lord unashamed. His redemptive act for believers shall be immortalized incorruptible at the instance of Rapture. {ESV}

Any caught unaware in sin shall be devastated and desperate for the Lord's benevolent promise to 'wipe away all tears.' This shall include those of sin-filled shame, having been caught in the very act, per I John 2:28, "And now, little children, abide in him; that, when he shall appear, we may have confidence, and not be ashamed before him at his coming." {KJV}

Once more, Paul admonishes the Ephesians in 4:30, "And do not grieve the Holy Spirit of God, by whom you were sealed for the day of redemption." This sealing of salvation is eternal and cannot be corrupted. Having been divinely assured through God's Holy Word of our eternal security in Him, we must ever be mindful to meet Him at any moment. For, not only shall we be ashamed to meet Jesus with unconfessed sin, so we shall grieve Him at first blush, even as we grieve Him now in the flesh when we fall into sin.

Returning to the imminent Rapture even as he closes his letter in Eph. 5:27, Paul snapshots this meeting in the air, "...that He might present her to Himself a glorious church..." Note Jesus is at once preparing his Bride that He might present her to *Himself without spot or wrinkle*. {NKJV}

Acts

Our literary timeline for the imminent Rapture now advances to 62 a.d. when the Apostle Luke penned the historical book of Acts. Our focus on the imminence of the Rapture here rests on Jesus' ascension in Chapter One.

(This is a perfect passage to contemplate an essential, and extremely useful rule of prophecy interpretation. It has been stated through the years and may be simply rendered thus: When a passage makes literal sense, one need not search any further.)

Consider: Acts 1:10-11 – "And while they looked steadfastly toward heaven as He went up, behold, two men stood by them in white apparel, who also said, 'Men of Galilee, why do you stand gazing up into heaven?

"This same Jesus, who was taken up from you into heaven, will so come in like manner as you saw Him go into heaven." {NKJV}

Upon His resurrection and then following 40 days of instruction and fellowship, Jesus led the disciples to the Mount of Olives to witness His ascension into Heaven. Having finished His final revelations, Jesus began to ascend into the clouds. The disciples were mesmerized, understandably. And while they were in this transfixion there were two men, apparently angels by their garb and appearance, who told the disciples this same Jesus, who was being taken up into heaven in their sight, would be returning in like manner as they were seeing Him depart.

Jesus describes the Son of Man returning in Matthew 24 to the earth itself. Here they describe Him returning in like manner, in the clouds, which agrees with Matthew 24:30 as, "...they shall see the Son of man coming in the clouds of heaven with power and great glory." This would then describe His return to the earth, "...immediately after the tribulation of those days..." {Matt. 24:29}. Therefore, this reference is unquestionably following the wrath of God that has been poured out upon the earth dwellers. Judgment now intensifies with His Bride, who has returned at Jesus' side, Rev. 19, witnessing.

Seeing Jesus return in the clouds prohibits connecting Acts 1:9 with I Thess. 4:17. Paul states believers shall be caught up into the clouds. There is no indication as yet discovered in Scripture that Jesus will be visible at the Rapture to any but those going up. The Acts passage, as well as Revelation, has Jesus descending to the earth, at the end of the Tribulation. {KJV}

Lest any suspect this interpretation is placing too fine a point on the verses in question may Matt. 5:18 be submitted in support, "For truly I tell you, until heaven and earth disappear, not the smallest letter, not the least stroke of a pen, will by any means disappear from the Law until everything is accomplished." {NIV}

Should doubts linger, II Tim. 3:16-17 may be useful as added confirmation, "All Scripture is breathed out by God and profitable for teaching, for reproof, for correction, and for training in righteousness, that the man of God may be complete, equipped for every good work." {ESV}

This reflected consummation of wrath that Paul had aforehand instructed in I Thess. 1:10, that God would deliver believers from, precedes Jesus' return to the earth. I Thess. 5:9 clarifies God has not appointed believers to this wrath, but to salvation.

And Paul himself was waiting for the Lord's imminent deliverance, as the Thessalonians had been doing for over a decade when Acts was written. He states in I Thess. 4:17 speaking of "...we who are alive and remain shall be caught up together with them (the dead in Christ just made alive), in the clouds to meet the Lord in the air." May we emphasize we shall be meeting Jesus '...*in the clouds*...*" (unseen!),* not on the ground! {NASB}

In earnest, allow me to expand on this truth speaking of going up into the clouds. A man striving to argue against the Rapture doctrine challenged that the I Thess. passage did not say which direction those raptured would travel. He was quickly informed verse 17 proclaims believers shall be '...caught <u>up</u>...*in the clouds*...' {KJV} He was asked what direction he might think that *'up'* would be? No response was given.

To be fair, Philip's catching away from the Ethiopian eunuch in Acts 8:39 only notes he went 'away.' But Jerome's Vulgate again captures the third person indicative for 'rapio,' 'rapuit', showing Philip was violently 'snatched away' by the Holy Spirit instantaneously from that scene when his work was done.

A standing joke among Bible school students has been that Acts was the only unfinished book in the New Testament. The implication being that until Jesus calls us home at the Rapture, we shall continue to 'redeem the time' as we 'press toward the mark of the upward call', 'occupying until He comes', 'having done all,' to 'stand fast' 'watching & waiting' to be 'delivered' out of 'this present evil age.'

As the chronicling of Acts reveals, and as this study confirms, though the leaders of the church believed, taught, and practiced the imminence of the Rapture, their theological position not only did not sway them from fulfilling Jesus' command to make disciples of all nations, but rather compelled them even more earnestly to redeem the time in doing so.

Knowing that Jesus was 'at the door' inspired them to press hard on being faithful to His commands. Paul instructed, "But you, keep your head in all situations, endure hardship, do the work of an evangelist, discharge all the duties of your ministry." {II Tim. 4:5, NIV}

Acts itself, as the apostles and followers continued serving, steadfast and abounding in His work, documents the perseverance that must be exemplified to all who call upon the Lord, to preach the word, being instant in season and out, for God shall make a short work.

In fact, two years of activity follow before the next five epistles are even written according to historical record. Unlike the modern Christian publishing world, awash in a torrent of offerings, in the beginning years of the Church, publication was performed out of necessity rather than for monetary gain. We believers of this present age must be as circumspect in our outreach.

Philippians

Also written in 64 a.d., Paul's letter to the Philippians employs the term 'the day of Jesus Christ' or 'the day of Christ,' referring to the Rapture. Twice in Chapter One, verses 6 & 10, actions are described '...until the day of Jesus Christ...'

The apostle looks to rejoicing in that 'day' in 2:16. And encourages, "...be found in Him...' in 3:9-11. This can only be on that 'day' since the service of all saints, the risen dead and we who remain, culminates in that 'day' which has been noted in Chapter One.

And perhaps the most revealing passage concerning the imminent Rapture in all of the Bible is cast in Chapter Three. We read:

> *Philipp. 3:13-14: "Brothers, I do not consider that I have made it my own. But one thing I do: forgetting what lies behind and straining forward to what lies ahead, I press on toward the goal <u>for the prize of the upward call</u> of God in Christ Jesus." {ESV}*

Here Paul declares his pre-eminent, motivating force and drive of ministry, the prize of the promised 'upward call of God in Christ Jesus.' He seeks with all his heart to win the crown proclaimed in II Tim. 4:8d to '…all those who have loved His appearing…'

Paul was educated by the Lord Himself in the Rapture doctrine, per I Thess. 4:15a, "We tell you this directly from the Lord: We who are still living when the Lord returns will not meet him ahead of those who have died." {NLT}

Notice at this point Paul is under the impression that he will remain alive on earth until the Rapture, "we… who are left until the coming of the Lord…" It becomes apparent God reveals specific details in His time. Four years after writing Philippians, seventeen years following I Thess., pass before Paul understands he has been moved to depart as he writes to Timothy, "…I have finished my course…" {I Thess. 4:15, ESV; II Tim. 4:7b, KJV}

But what is Paul's perspective as he writes to the Philippians in this prison moment? From whence does the apostle strain toward his ultimate goal, Eph. 2:6, "And he has raised us up with him and seated us with himself in Heaven in Yeshua the Messiah." Paul comforts himself in his Heavenly position which already awaits him. (ABPE)

Maintaining this view Paul affirms in Philipp. 3:20, "For our citizenship is in heaven, *from which we also eagerly wait for the Savior*, the Lord Jesus Christ." And it must be repeated, Paul **_eagerly_** awaits the Shout! This is no momentary, or diversionary teaching. The imminent Rapture is not merely 'filler' doctrine to help bide the time of passage through this veil of tears. {NKJV}

A confirmation has already been given by Paul, initially in I Thess. 4:16, in which he prophesies the raising of those dead in Christ at the Rapture *first*. And then here in Philip. 3:11, "that by any means possible I may attain the resurrection from the dead." This place of honor reserved unto all that shall be transformed into 'the first load,' as Paul described the dead rising first. {ESV}

We already know from Thessalonians Paul was teaching the dead in Christ would be raised first at the Rapture. And that at that point in time he was counting himself as among 'we who are alive and remain.' Yet roughly 13 years later, Paul is 'now' striving to be with the first load going in the Rapture, *'by any means' possible*. {Philipp. 3:11, NKJV}

Colossians

Colossians is yet another of the four prison epistles written in 64 a.d., (included with Ephesians, Philippians and Philemon), in which the last Apostle once again confirms the reality of the Rapture or Blessed Hope. Paul highlights this fact in 3:4 – "When Christ who is our life appears, then you also will appear with Him in glory." {*The Second Coming*!} Yes, Jesus is coming back to the earth and his appearance, by His own word, shall be as lightning flashing from the east to the west! Every eye on earth shall see Him! And when He appears, you who believe in Him will also appear *with* Him in glory!

And how else could you be with Him, except that you had been raptured!

Paul's 'Philemon' letter, penned in this same time frame, does not mention the imminent Rapture. The apostle does fulfill his own admonition of Gal. 6:10, "Therefore, as we have opportunity, let us do good to all people, *especially* to those who belong to the family of believers." This displays another Christian duty Jesus desires to find his followers enacting when He calls us out! {NIV}

To continue, obviously, we couldn't be returning with Him unless we had gone to Him at an earlier time. But yet even more personal is the reference to the Rapture. For Paul was writing to the Colossians directly. And he was encouraging them that they, the Colossians, should expect to be with Jesus when He appears.

Again, Paul is envisioning an imminent event, per James and Peter. The Judge is at the door! While Paul is stating we shall be with Jesus when He returns! {James 5:9, I Peter 4:7, GNV}

How should we in today's Body, two millennia later, be postured in reference to Jesus calling us out? Expectant! Eager! Paul has already proclaimed that '... we who are alive and remain...' are going to immediately follow the dead in Christ up to meet Jesus in the air.

Truthfully, it has been nearly 2,000 years since these words were written! But each generation must navigate its own time. Reflecting our first century, initial generation of believers, we must mirror their lives. We must strive to stay fresh, keep our lamps lit, our wicks trimmed and our lamps burning bright! He is coming at any moment, while it is still called 'today.'

Paul turns to leadership responsibility in the body as the reader looks to Chapter four of Colossians, invoking the title 'Masters,' as he begins. One cannot but acknowledge in a study of this intent the closeness of such a fulfilling. It was after all Jesus Himself that, speaking of the end of the age, warned against *the* Chief Master returning to find those in authority mistreating their charges. And so, the importance and relevance of this instruction is perfectly understood to its depths.

But in particular, the prophecy student must focus on 4:3, as Paul implores his brethren specifically to pray for him, "...that God would open to us a door for the word, to speak the mystery of Christ, for which I am also in chains." {NKJV}

Paul could have easily attributed his imprisonment to the proclamation of the Gospel, which is the power of God unto salvation, to the Jew first and also to the Greek as he points out in Romans 1:16. Rather the Apostle declares his chains are also a result of, and a demand for his liberation to proclaim the mystery of Christ! What mystery is Paul referring to?

There are many mysteries related to Jesus that are recorded throughout scripture. Combined, they are in their totality the Mystery of Christ. We shall continue to focus on this one prophecy, which is any moment now going to erupt!

I Cor. 15:51-53, spotlights the heart of Paul's goal revealed in his Philippians claim, "Behold, I *tell* you a <u>*mystery*</u>: We shall not all sleep, but we shall *all* be changed – in a moment, in the twinkling of an eye, at the last trumpet. For the trumpet will sound, and the dead will be raised incorruptible, and we shall be changed. For this corruptible must put on incorruption, and this mortal must put on immortality." {NKJV}

Was this mystery of the Rapture what Paul was referring to? Context divulges the answer. This was the mystery of the *imminent* Rapture.

True, the imminent Rapture mystery is merely only one of the hidden riches of Christ. Matt. 13:11 speaks of the mysteries of Heaven. Paul was striving to preach to as many as he knew, though he only knew in part. Yet, the one thing he was doing overall, was pressing towards "...

the prize of the upward call…" of Jesus. {NKJV; Philipp. 3:14, ESV}

God's reason for giving Paul such impetus to focus on the Rapture was because it is imminent to the entire body of Christ. Paul formulated the posture earnest Christians should emulate! Nothing else is required to be fulfilled. It shall transpire at any given moment. And the longer time continues the greater increase of tension on the fulfillment of this prophecy. Thus, it always excites, it always strengthens, it always comforts.

Once more, as Paul again employs 'finally', in closing a letter, he encourages the Colossians with our Blessed Hope in 4:2-4, "Continue earnestly in prayer, being vigilant in it with thanksgiving; meanwhile praying also for us, that God would open to us a door for the word, to speak the mystery *{hidden truth}* of Christ, for which I am also in chains, that I might make it manifest, as I ought to speak." {NKJV}

Even if Paul were speaking generally of the mystery of Christ, wouldn't Jesus' *imminent* appearing be prioritized by order at the top of that list?

Paul prophesies, "Behold, I shew you a mystery…" Nearly five years later Paul declares in Philippians that his one goal is in *pressing toward the 'upward call'* of Christ Jesus. The imminent Rapture was therefore Paul's impetus to serving the Lord. This in order that His personal work would then continue with the proper tension. For Paul testified, "¹⁴ Clearly, Christ's love guides us. We are convinced of the fact that one man has died for all people. Therefore, all people have died." That love reaches its zenith at His Shout! {II Cor. 5:14, GWT}

We know none are promised tomorrow, and delay courts eternal disaster. These are true. But pre-eminently as we believers anticipate His Shout, we fulfill Isaiah 26:3, "You keep him in perfect peace whose mind is stayed on you, because he trusts in you." He truly is our Hope and Joy. {ESV}

Hebrews

Hebrews, also written in a.d. 64, spotlights the imminence of the Rapture. Unavoidable insight is gained reading 9:28 in which that writer proclaims "...so Christ was offered once to bear the sins of many. *To those who eagerly wait for Him He will appear a second time apart from sin, for salvation."* {NKJV}

Debate still swirls around the naming of who may have written Hebrews. For the record, this writer holds with the Pauline school. Whoever the author of this epistle might be, the reference in this passage is clear, and must be highlighted.

First, Jesus will appear a second time in the present tense of those 'who eagerly wait for Him.' No mention of when, yet one cannot escape Paul's admonition, "... while it is still called *today...*" when calling all to repentance. For the Hebrews author notes Jesus will appear '*apart from sin, for salvation.*' Even the five wise virgins come easily to mind in this statement.

Imminence shades other teachings as well, foreshadowing the mind of God in 10:13 of this letter, "From henceforth (vs. 12...after he had offered one sacrifice for sins forever...) *expecting* till his enemies be made his footstool." (The use of 'expecting,' demonstrates the continuity of maintaining a continuous, vigilant, anticipatory watch, thus inculcating the understanding of 'imminence' into even this use of the present tense of 'expecting.') {KJV}

An even more titillating reference appears in verse 25 of this same chapter 10. Many congregations have heard the exhortation to faithful attendance at church meetings in the preached message, "Not forsaking the assembling of ourselves together," {note: the emphasis on *'ourselves'* showing all believers are responsible}. And often the plea is left here. But, continuing on in the verse we read, "… as the manner of some is; but exhorting one another: and *so much the more, as ye see the day approaching."* "Ye" given as an individual, personal responsibility. (KJV}

Incredibly, the writer reveals expectancy that some certain generation who read these words shall even see 'the day' approaching around them. At the very least, 'the day' encompasses the culmination of all things as Jesus returns. But in context, the Hebrews author has just a few verses earlier spoken of '…those who <u>eagerly</u> wait for Him…' And, again, Jesus had warned in Luke 21:36 of those '…worthy to escape all these things that shall come to pass…'

Keeping in mind Paul's emphasis on 'today', the writer of Hebrews clarifies the waiting time in 10:37, *"For yet a little while, and He that shall come will come, and will not tarry."* Jesus will be calling his Bride out in *just a little while*, He is at the door, and He will not tarry! Waiting will be no more when He comes back! {KJV}

Hebrews 11:5 "…translation…" melds seamlessly with the earlier I Cor. 15:53, as the 'taking' of Enoch is revealed in the imminent "corruptible must put on incorruption…" as believers change in the twinkling of an eye!

*By faith Enoch was translated that he should
not see death; and was not found, because God
had translated him: for before his translation he
had this testimony, that he pleased God. {Heb.
11:5, KJV}*

*Again, we see the emphasis of 'faith', returning us to
Paul's Philippian admonition.*

I Timothy

And in that same year, Paul pens another reminder in I
Tim. 6:14, "...that you keep this commandment without
spot, blameless until our Lord Jesus Christ's appearing
..." (See entire passage of 6:11-16) {NKJV}

Paul's opening salutation to Timothy had re-pinned
the focus he'd attested to in Philippians, "Paul, an apostle
of Jesus Christ by the commandment of God our Saviour,
and Lord Jesus Christ, *which is our 'hope' (anticipation);*" {I Tim. 1:1, Au-KJV}

Specifically, though certainly all believers are to be
recipients of this exhortation, Paul warns in verse 6:11,
"But thou, O man of God, flee these things; and follow
after righteousness, godliness, faith, love, patience, meekness. Fight the good fight of faith, lay hold on eternal life,
whereunto thou art also called, and hast professed a good
profession before many witnesses." {KJV}

Paul has just been emphasizing the deceitfulness of
riches and in 6:14, admonishes those who have ears to
hear of the importance of needed holiness at Messiah's
calling out, "...until the appearing of our Lord Jesus
Christ." {KJV}

Once more the self-proclaimed 'least of all Apostles' emphasizes the very imminence of our Lord's snatching out His Bride!

Chapter Twelve

Pleasing God

a.d. 64-65–Titus
a.d. 66–Jude
a.d. 68–II Timothy

Three epistles that deal directly with the imminence of the Rapture are accounted for during the last years leading to the Roman sacking of Jerusalem in 70 a.d. Jesus always keeps the best for last. These final encouragements are no different.

Titus

In 65 a.d., Paul again illustrates the immediacy and imminence of the Rapture in Titus 2:11-15:

> *"For the grace of God that brings salvation has appeared to all men, teaching us that, denying ungodliness and worldly lusts, we should live soberly, righteously, and godly in the present age,* **looking for the blessed hope, and the glorious appearing of our great God and Savior Jesus**

__Christ__, who gave Himself for us, that He might redeem us from every lawless deed and purify for Himself His own special people, zealous for good works. Speak these things, exhort, and rebuke with all authority. Let no one despise you." {NKJV}

Once again the event of the Rapture is couched in the terms of present tense, 'looking' for the Blessed Hope and the glorious appearing of our Great God and Savior Jesus Christ.' Note especially also: This passage repeats the active voice described in I John 3:3, as we continue anticipating the Rapture. This 'looking' for His snatching us out, is the very action itself which *purifies* us.

As we eagerly await His calling out, anticipating His Trumpet and our change from mortal to immortal, our striving against sin on a daily basis, moment to moment battling and denying ungodliness and worldly lusts, we move soberly through this present age. Living godly lives starkly emphasizes all testimony to the world that He is coming at any moment.

This drawing near to the Lord and His holiness cannot be overstated. It is this moment to moment battle which in fact illustrates the purpose of the imminent Rapture. Not only does no man know the day or the hour, but more specifically, no one knows the very moment of His Shout! "Be ye also ready..." takes on new impact!

Not incidentally, Paul continues to identify the person of Jesus of Nazareth as 'our Great God and Savior Jesus Christ.' As throughout the Tanakh and the Brit Chadashah, the old and new Testaments, Paul here re-emphasizes the Deity of Jesus, and His position as Savior of the world, stressing the personhood of Jesus.

Jude

Our next reference to the imminent Rapture is given by Jude, the half-brother of Jesus (see Matthew 13:55– 'Judas'), in the epistle he wrote in a.d. 66.

This is a remarkable epistle for several reasons. First, of course, is that the author identifies himself as the full brother of James, who so introduced, can only be the epistle author of the same name, Galatians 1:19 and 2:9, the first pastor of the Jerusalem congregation, most significantly the half-brother of Jesus our Messiah. Thus, Jude establishes his own personal, two-fold familial connection with our Savior.

He opens his letter by explaining he intended to write concerning 'our common salvation,' that most precious gift each of us in the Body of Messiah share. 'Common' referring to equally shared, not as in 'ordinary.' How could eternal salvation ever be 'ordinary'?

But Divine compunction to address false teaching forces Jude to alter his tack.

"Beloved, although I was very eager to write to you about our common salvation, I found it necessary to write appealing to you to contend for the faith that was once for all delivered to the saints. For certain people have crept in unnoticed who long ago were designated for this condemnation, ungodly people, who pervert the grace of our God into sensuality and deny our only Master and Lord, Jesus Christ." {Jude, verses 3-4, ESV}

"Certain people have crept in unnoticed," heretical teachers, justifying and legitimizing sexual sin! Search 'sensuality' for confirmation.

Jude exhorts believers to a defense of the faith '... once for all delivered to the saints." {Jude 3-4, NKJV}

By itself, this admonition confirms the duty of each believer to contend, compete, and stand for Biblical doctrine against false teachers especially those within the Body.

A brief historical perspective is reported which goes back to the Exodus and further to Genesis and the early generations of Adam.

Jude returns the reader to the consideration of Enoch, the man who walked with God and was not. "Now, Enoch, the seventh from Adam, prophesied about these men also, saying, 'behold the Lord comes with ten thousand of His saints, to execute judgment on all, to convict all who are ungodly among them of all their ungodly deeds which they have committed in an ungodly way, and of all the harsh things which ungodly sinners have spoken against Him (God).'" Note the four references to the 'ungodly.' No confusion here. {Jude 14-15, NKJV}

This passage begins by substantiating the teaching of the Rapture, ensuring His saints will be _with_ Jesus at His Return. His purpose in returning is to first and foremost save Israel through the intervention and destruction of their enemies; and then to levy judgment on the ungodly, especially those ungodly sinners that have spoken against Him. This last brings immediately and unavoidably to mind the atheists of this world.

Having thus reminded the reader of the Return of the Lord Jesus to judge the world in verses 14-15, Jude himself points to the positive discipline of anticipating

Jesus' calling out His Bride in verse 21, "...looking for the mercy of our Lord Jesus Christ, unto eternal life." Here, once more, the believer is implored to be 'looking for' Jesus to appear at any moment, not in wrath, but in mercy!

And, excitingly, it is impossible to avoid bringing to mind Lamentations 3:21-26:

> *"This I recall to my mind; therefore, I have hope. Through the Lord's mercies we are not consumed. Because His compassions fail not. They are new every morning; great is your faithfulness. The Lord is my portion, says my soul, therefore I hope in Him! The Lord is good to those who wait for Him, to the soul who seeks Him. It is good that one should hope and wait quietly, for the salvation of the Lord." {NKJV}*

Here, over five centuries before Paul reveals the mystery of the imminent Rapture in I Cor. 15:51-52, Jeremiah is moved by the Ruach Ha Kodesh, the Holy Spirit, our Comforter, to foreshadow the teaching of the comfort of the Lord, His promise to bring us to Him before the Great Tribulation begins!

And folded within this prophetic blessing is the reminder of imminence, for the reader is assured that the Lord's mercy is *'new every morning.'* Every new day presents the next opportunity of God's 'any moment' calling out!

How perfectly woven is God's Holy Scripture, that in the midst of Lamentation the weeping prophet is catapulted to the Heights of God's Mercies. From this encouragement to 'hope and wait quietly for the Lord,' one recognizes Paul's I Thess. 4:11 instruction to 'study to be quiet.' "The heart of the godly thinks carefully before speaking..." Knowing the sureness of God's promises, we anticipate in comfort and strength, quietly waiting in study to hear His Shout! {Prov. 15:28, NLT}

Even as Jesus' half-brother, Jude, comforts and encourages believers of our return to earth with Jesus to execute judgment upon all, Jeremiah is lifted to joyful hope as God reveals His never-ending faithfulness and mercy.

And God hints to Jeremiah of the imminence of the Rapture as He proclaims His Mercy is new every morning. Yes, as Peter and James declared, Jesus is at the door. While it is still called today, Paul remonstrates, do not harden your hearts, and receive His Mercy! Be ready for His calling out! Behold, the Bride Groom cometh!

Importantly we in our present generation witness in these passages the constant attention of the first generation of believers from the very founding of the Church, cultivating anticipation for the calling out by Jesus. Jude's exhortation to be 'looking for the mercy of the Lord," echoes both the eager anticipation encouraged, and the imminence expected.

Eph. 3:20 contextually confirms God's ability to perform this miracle, "Now to him who is able to do far more abundantly than all that we ask or think, according to the power at work within us..." {ESV}

Jude closes with this defining reality, verse 24, "Now to him who is able to keep you from stumbling and *to present you* blameless before the presence of his glory with great joy..." Col. 1:22, "...*to present you* holy, and blameless, and above reproach in His sight," with Eph. 5:27 mirroring the image, "...that He might *present her* to Himself a glorious church..." {ESV, Modern English Version, NKJV}

How should we then anticipate this great event? The Lord is good to those who wait for Him, who seek Him. It is good that one should hope and quietly wait for the salvation of the Lord.

When? Now. In this present moment, as He shall call us out! We should constantly be looking for His mercy. And it is newly fresh every morning! It is going to be at any moment, while it is still called 'today'!

II Timothy

In the late sixties of the first century, around the spring of a.d. 68, the Apostle Paul was sentenced to death by Emperor Nero at the chopping block for preaching the Gospel: The death, burial, and resurrection of Jesus Christ. {I Cor. 15:1-4}

Paul confesses in II Tim. 1:12, "For the which cause I also suffer these things: nevertheless, I am not ashamed: for I know whom I have believed and am persuaded that he is able to keep that which I have committed unto him against that day." {KJV}

What was the reason? 1:10 reveals, "But is now made manifest by the appearing of our Savior Jesus Christ..." Was Paul making a connection between the Gospel, the death, burial and resurrection of Jesus, and the imminent Rapture? Paul, here, is referencing Jesus 'appearing' in the present tense, as he has so often done before. {KJV}

Yet, one must surmise from scriptural evidences, that Paul is acknowledging, first of all, that Jesus 'is'! Jesus rose from the dead, appeared to over 500 witnesses at once, appeared to Paul on the Damascus road, and raptured Paul to heaven as Paul wrote, so this apostle can only think of Jesus in the present tense !

And, as he did in I Thessalonians, Paul here intermingles the Gospel, in verse 10, with Jesus' appearing. Verse 10 continues, "...who hath abolished death, and hath brought life and immortality to light through the Gospel."

Compare I Thess. 4:14, "For if we believe that Jesus died and rose again, even so them also which sleep in Jesus will God bring with him." Mark also the resurrection report used here by Paul to undergird foundationally the teaching of the imminent Rapture. Paul asserts that if we Christians do believe that Jesus died and rose again, which is imperative if we are to call ourselves Christians, then we can be assured that Jesus will bring all who are dead in Him when He comes to receive us unto Himself! {KJV}

Which explains why the Rapture would be foremost on the Apostle's mind at this point, for he is preparing to submit to decapitation for his beliefs! What a marvelous future he has to look forward to! His own bodily resurrection at the Shout! He could be among the first of the first to be resurrected! And as he has pointed to continually throughout his epistles, we shall be with Paul as his joy and crown.

As Paul prays a blessing of mercy on the house of Onesiphorus, he expands the request in 1:18, "The Lord grant to him that he may find mercy from the Lord in that Day..." {NKJV}

Here the reader is reminded and returned to the topic of God's mercy, that which was encouraged to be sought for by Jude, and that which was revealed to Jeremiah as new every morning. This must be looking ultimately to the Day of Christ, the Rapture, for again, believers, dead and alive, are not appointed unto wrath.

Paul returns to the theme of 'faith' in II Tim. 2, bringing into remembrance the admonition from Hebrews concerning Enoch, that without faith it is impossible to please God. Jesus proclaims in Matthew 12:30, "He who is not with me is against me; and he who does not gather with me scatters abroad," emphasizing everything in life is related to Him. {NKJV}

Paul continues, 2:11-13 – "This is a faithful saying: For if we died with Him, we shall also live with Him. If we endure, we shall also reign with Him. If we deny Him, He also will deny us. If we are faithless, He remains faithful; He cannot deny Himself." {NKJV}

Jesus cannot deny Himself or His word. Thus, our faith is of Him! "For it is by grace you have been saved, through faith—and this is not from yourselves, it is the gift of God—not by works, so that no one can boast." He it is that we trust, and in His Word, "For in him we live and move and have our being," as Paul preached. {Eph. 2:8-9; Acts 17:28a, NIV}

It cannot be too strongly stated here that our 'being' does not end at the grave as some would claim. Pointedly, Paul is writing this second epistle to Timothy in view of his own approaching execution. His faith is not in himself, but rather in Jesus and the Word of God as the apostle stated in I Thess. 4:15a, "For this we say to you by the word of the Lord..." Paul is emphasizing that the word he is giving to the Thessalonians is not his own concocted idea, but he is simply relaying to them what Jesus has given him to preach. {NASB}

Now, in the opening of his concluding remarks to Timothy, Paul once more charges Timothy to preach the Word of God, to be instant in season and out. And Paul's goad is the reminder in II Tim. 4:1-2 of the Bema seat for all believers following the imminent Rapture, Jesus' appearance in the air. Intriguingly, Paul even includes the reminder by his authoritative choice of the present tense imminent Rapture as supported in Timothy's charge:

"I charge thee therefore before God, and the Lord Jesus Christ, who shall judge the quick and the dead at his appearing and his kingdom; Preach the word; be instant in season, out of season; reprove, rebuke, exhort with all longsuffering and doctrine." {II Tim 4:1-2, KJV}

So, Paul, who has undergirded his proclamation of the imminent Rapture in I Thess. 4:14 upon the declaration of the death and resurrection of Jesus, now employs the doctrine of the imminent Rapture to deploy encouragement to preach the Gospel itself!

All the more reason for the 'least of the Apostles' to heighten the charge to immediacy in verse two, proclaiming, "...be instant, in season and out..." If the Rapture is set for any moment of the day that is called 'today,' one is obligated to be 'instant'!

Also note 'by his appearing.' This perspective blends superbly with Paul's proclamation of I Thess. 4:14, "For since we believe that Jesus died and rose again, even so, through Jesus, God will bring with him those who have fallen asleep." For as Paul undergirds the preaching of the doctrine of the imminence of the Rapture with the death and resurrection of Jesus, so here, he inflames the urgency of preaching the word of God and His imminent appearance. {ESV}

And so, we arrive at the capstone of Paul's teaching on the imminence of the Rapture. Here, in II Tim. 4:8, Paul shares with Timothy his view of future reward. "Finally, there is laid up for me the crown of righteousness, which the Lord, the righteous Judge, will give to me on that Day, and not to me only but also to all who have loved His appearing." {NKJV}

Preparing for his execution by decapitation, Paul ironically encourages first himself on the crown that Jesus is going to bestow on him at that Day. Faith! What day is that? Look to 1:12, picking up at, "and am persuaded that He is able to keep that which I have committed unto Him against that Day." Again, a specific 'Day' is called to mind. In James 1:12 we find, "Blessed is the one who perseveres under trial because, having stood the test, that person will receive the crown of life that the Lord has promised to those who love him." And what then is the promise James is referring to? Revelation 22:12 reveals the answer, "Look, I am coming soon! My reward is with me, and I will give to each person according to what they have done." {KJV, NIV}

But how do we know this relates to the imminent Rapture? Because we know James and Peter have stated that Jesus is 'at the door.' Paul has emphasized He is coming in the moment and space of time identified as in the 'present,' also for "…we who remain…" Additionally, Paul emphasized the need to repent, '…while it is still called today." And since the Tribulation is marked at seven years in length, and God has not appointed us unto wrath, we must be called out before the beginning of that trial that is going to fall upon the whole earth.

But Paul doesn't stop at encouraging himself. He emphasizes, "…and not to me only but also to all who have loved His appearing."

This returns the study to Paul's instruction on running the race to win the prize. He has noted that all run, but only one wins. The one in this case are all that love and anticipate His Shout! All who have trusted in Jesus for salvation will go in the Rapture, but only those who have loved and anticipated His calling out shall receive the crown!

Pointedly it must be emphasized, one need not be alive and anticipating His Shout when the Rapture occurs to receive the crown. One only has to have loved His appearing during their lives, during their watch, in order to receive the crown of righteousness!

Paul testifies he will receive the crown that Day of Christ! The Bema will be that Day!

Paul testifies to his faith in the Lord's deliverance again as he begins his closing remarks to his young soldier, II Tim. 4:18, "And the Lord will deliver me from every evil work and preserve me for His heavenly kingdom. To Him be glory forever and ever. Amen!" {NKJV}

Immediately one recalls Paul's remark in his Corinthian dissertation on the imminent Rapture in I Cor. 15:55, "O death, where is thy sting? O grave, where is thy victory?" For Paul knows he will be delivered from this evil work approaching him, and he will be preserved from the sting of death, and the grave shall not hold him in its cold compress. For he had announced in I Thess. 4:16, some 15 years prior, "For the Lord himself will come down from heaven, with a loud command, with the voice of the archangel and with the trumpet call of God, and the dead in Christ will rise first." {KJV, NIV}

How long will Paul have to wait for his bodily transformation? Jesus is at the door!

So, Paul is only receiving one more blessed promotion from God. Paul will also be receiving the Martyr's crown. Not insubstantially, Paul is also being given cuts to go to the front of the line, for now he is looking forward to being among the very first that Jesus receives unto Himself! And he is looking forward from his seat in Heaven!

Chapter Thirteen

Final Words

---

a.d. 90-96–I John
a.d. 90-96–II John
a.d. 90-96–III John
a.d. 96–Revelation

Accepting traditional dating aids in supporting the imminent Rapture study. As we can see, focusing on publication dates, establishing when various concepts are first issued, does allow a better grasp of the perspectives on prophecy. In a word, who believed what; where did they believe it; when did they believe; why did they believe it; and/ how did they believe it?

This said, there appears to be a span of three decades between Paul's final prison letter to Timothy, a.d. 68, and John's a.d. writings in the 90's. These include John's epistles I, II, & III, and his closing with the Book of Revelation.

Use of these dating's bring together three important understandings more closely coordinated with a view of the imminent Rapture. That view blends with present day preaching acceptance that first generation Christians did believe, teach, and practice the daily anticipation of the imminent Rapture. That would include the last living Apostle and New Testament author, John the Apostle. "One of them, the disciple whom Jesus loved, was reclining next to him." {John 13:23, NIV}

Yet even setting aside the dating question momentarily, a reader can only omit the proclaimed imminent Rapture from first generation Christian practice by marring Holy Writ. As the myriad of preceding quotes in this book substantiate compellingly the New Testament is replete with imminent Rapture references.

I John

John establishes in his first letter that his testimony encompasses the time from the beginning of Jesus' ministry. He undergirds this proclamation by declaring believers are extant that have heard with their own ears, seen with their very eyes, looked upon, not merely caught glimpses of, and have physically touched with their very own hands individually the Word of life, Jesus Christ, Yeshua Ha Maschiach. {I John, 1:1-3}

Narrowing our focus, we return to the subject of eschatology, or the study of last things, beginning in I John 2:18 and following as John enters into the reality of the imminent Rapture:

"Little children, it is the last hour..." John establishes. He does not just suggest believers are in the last day, but even the very final hour before the Lord calls out His children as Paul promised by '...word of the Lord.' Once again, the imminence is brought to the fore, as John telescopes into the 'last hour'. Getting exciting, no? {I Thess. 4:15}

Peter has made it clear that one day is with the Lord as a thousand years and a thousand years as one day. This recalls Hosea's revelation that the Lord would return on the third day to rescue Israel.

Who on earth can deny that life is truly *'swifter than a weaver's shuttle'* as Job testified? "My days are swifter than a weaver's shuttle, and they come to an end without hope." Chillingly, the mystery of hope Paul revealed is absent in Job's despair! Our anticipation of the Blessed Hope was yet to be proclaimed! Even so, mysteriously, Job declares his faith that his Redeemer lives and will stand again upon the earth. {Job 7:6, NIV}

A more shockingly positive testimony has since been bestowed on we who are today trusting in the Holy One of Israel! "But let me reveal to you a wonderful secret. We will not all die, but we will all be transformed! It will happen in a moment, in the blink of an eye, when the last trumpet is blown. For when the trumpet sounds, those who have died will be raised to live forever. And we who are living will also be transformed." {I Cor. 15:51-52, NLT}

Grasping that truth, how easily then can one glance over the past centuries to Paul's pronouncement. That was two millennia ago! Tell me that time doesn't fly!

Perceptively the reader concludes John's perspective is therefore divinely accurate. John understands Jesus is at the door.

And thus, the disciple whom Jesus loved brings his little children into present reality, I John 2:28, "And now, little children, abide in Him, ***that when He appears, we may have confidence and not be ashamed before Him at His coming."*** {NKJV}

'Now' John emphasizes. Not in the immediate future, but now, "...while it is called 'today'." 'Abide' John instructs. He doesn't ask that we enter into fellowship with Jesus, but rather that we maintain our spiritual bond with Him and 'abide' and live in this bond. And most importantly, as we are now abiding in Jesus, when He appears, He is going to appear in 'the now.' We should be expecting Him at 'any moment' now!

John first stipulates in this teaching verse that believers need to abide in Jesus in this 'now.' 'Abide' means to dwell with. We need to walk step by step through each day with Jesus, moment to moment. In this instance, John focuses on the 'why' of this practice. That when Jesus appears, and Jesus shall appear at the Rapture to all believers, those resurrected from the dead, and all we who are alive and yet remain on this earth, all may have confidence and not be ashamed before Him at His coming.

A significant factor in this verse is the warning to not be caught ashamed. There will be no crown for those caught ashamed. Jesus has paid for their sins, but they shall lose rewards they would have received for following Him.

The rewards are classified as gold, silver and precious stones. Worthless service, however, is promised, wood, hay and stubble.

"11 For other foundation can no man lay than that is laid, which is Jesus Christ. 12 Now if any man build upon this foundation gold, silver, precious stones, wood, hay, stubble; 13 every man's work shall be made manifest: for the day shall declare it, because it shall be revealed by fire; and the fire

shall try every man's work of what sort it is. ¹⁴ If any man's work abide which he hath built there-upon, he shall receive a reward. ¹⁵ If any man's work shall be burned, he shall suffer loss: but he himself shall be saved; yet so as by fire." I Cor. 3:11-15, Au-KJV

The writer of Hebrews encourages, "...But, beloved, we are persuaded better things of you..." Again, the imminent aspect of the Rapture drips from this warning. His nearness to appearance pre-figures our reception. When He appears, we who abide in Him shall in a twinkling be like Him! {Heb. 6:9, KJV}

Jesus amply alerts believers in the Gospels that we are to watch for His return because we are often reminded in many eschatological teachings, for some He shall come as 'a thief in the night.' Even though Jesus Himself accentuated this reality for those with ears to hear, the any moment promise is intended as a strength and comfort to all who believe and wait upon His word.

Although Jesus describes the convergence of world-wide, observable disasters in Luke 21:8-35, verse 36 is the focus Christians should be cultivating.

In verse 35 Jesus has already confirmed the trap the world will be caught in as these disasters proliferate. And He emphasizes these trials falling upon earth as a 'snare.'

But in verse 36 Jesus makes plain the Hope of the imminent Rapture:

"Watch ye, therefore, and pray always, that ye may be accounted worthy to escape all these things that shall come to pass, and to stand before the Son of man." {KJV}

Two important elements to take away from this pro-phetical encouragement are 1) Those found worthy shall escape world-wide disaster to receive the crown for anticipating, looking for and loving His appearing, and 2) All in Christ shall escape all these things that come upon the whole world.

Even with this amazing Hope, offered to all who will believe, there is that continuing warning of the thief in the night. Why? Due to the great percentage within Christendom that discounts this teaching. 'Multitudes' is an adequate accounting of all those who believe in Jesus and yet are unmindful of His elopement prepara-tions for them.

In Matt. 24:43, "But know this, that if the master of the house had known in what part of the night the thief was coming, he would have stayed awake and would not have let his house be broken into." Every eye is not going to see a thief approaching earth! Every eye will behold the King of Kings, and Lord of Lords descending with His Bride and His mighty army to save His children, Israel! {ESV}

Jesus elaborates in Luke, this time identifying the person in question as a servant of the returning Master:

"But and if that servant say in his heart, My lord delayeth his coming; and shall begin to beat the menservants and maidens, and to eat and drink, and to be drunken; The lord of that servant will come in a day when he looketh not for him, and at an hour when he is not aware, and will cut him in sunder, and will appoint him his portion with the unbelievers." {Luke 12:45-46, KJV}

II John

Lest confusion creep in, John confronts the misinterpretation that one might lose one's salvation in his very next letter, II John 1:8, NKJV, "Look to yourselves, that we do not lose those things we worked for, ***but that we may receive a full reward."*** Thus, we readily understand although we cannot lose our salvation (I John 5:13), we can suffer the loss of some, most, or even all of our rewards for which we labor. {KJV}

"If anyone's work is burned up, he will suffer loss, though he himself will be saved, but only as through fire." {I Cor. 3:15, ESV}

Horrifyingly worse, unbelievers have not only no reward to look forward to, they have only God's judgment in the fire to anticipate.

John highlights the glory of those rewards we shall receive in I John 3:2-3, "Beloved, now we are children of God; and it has not yet been revealed what we shall be, but we know that when He is revealed, we shall be like Him, for we shall see Him as He is. And everyone who has this hope* {*from the Greek for *'anticipation'*} in Him purifies himself, just as He is pure." {NKJV}

We do well to consider this prophetical promise from the vantage point of the imminent Rapture. Paul has declared in I Cor. 15:52 that we shall all be changed in a moment, in the twinkling of an eye, when this corruption shall put on incorruption, this mortal put on immortality.

In that moment when He is revealed we shall be like Him, as He is! An included strengthening is then prophesied, that "...everyone who has this hope (anticipation) in Him purifies himself, just as He is pure." Again, consider, we are not merely to meditate on these things, we are also to *anticipate* them!

III John

Third John does not mention the Rapture specifically. But verse 14 contains a perspective that cannot be overlooked in a study on the imminent, any moment Rapture.

"I hope to see you soon, and we will talk face to face. Peace to you. The friends here send their greetings. Greet the friends there by name. {NIV}"

John tells his readers that his temporal hope is to see them 'soon' in the physical world. Even at this late day in his life, the apostle continues to submit to the realities of this age. He anticipates seeing them '...face to face.' He sends the greetings of their friends. He sends greetings by name to those at the destination of this letter. *Anticipating the Rapture* *enhances* *his life in the present, it does not* *diminish* *it.*

Revelation

It is important in turning to the last book of the Bible to begin by authenticating the title. It is a singular word, *Apocalypse* in Greek, *Revelation* in the English. This book is therefore the revelation of Jesus Christ, by Jesus Himself, as He is now and forever! If you want to know who Jesus is, read this book of Revelation!

In order to produce an accurate encapsulation of history, past, present and future, Jesus oversees the narration of Revelation Himself.

Of major significance is Jesus' promise in 1:3 that all who **read** and **hear** the words of this book and **keep** these instructions shall receive a direct Divine Blessing for their efforts. Once again, notably, Jesus completes this verse by emphasizing *the time is at hand.*

It has been suggested by some Bible scholars that this proclamation of 'Blessing' is imagined by those who teach it. Rather, they opine, there is no special 'Blessing' declared here. Accepting the text as it is, thus astounds anyone presented with such observations. In the candor of this present age, this statement of Jesus Himself promising a special Blessing for all in obedience to His opening instructions 'for the time *is* at hand' simply *is what it is.*

"3 Blessed is he that readeth, and they that hear the words of this prophecy, and keep those things which are written therein: for the time is at hand." {Rev. 1:3, Au-KJV}

The Holy Bible is replete with the promises of Blessings to those who read and heed the Word of God! "I will worship toward thy holy temple and praise thy name for thy lovingkindness and for thy truth: for thou hast magnified thy word above all thy name." {Ps. 138:2, KJV}

The *immediacy* of this hour is emphasized continually throughout the 22 chapters of the Book of Revelation.

Exiled to the Isle of Patmos, a small island 32 miles west of Turkey in the Aegean Sea, around a.d. 96, by Emperor Domitian, for preaching the Gospel, John receives a vision from Jesus. Jesus tells John to write down the things "…which thou hast seen, and the things

which are, and the things which shall be hereafter..."
{Rev. 1:19, WBT}

At the risk of redundancy, for the purposes of this study, we shall be concentrating specifically on those elements related to the imminence of the Rapture as referenced in these pages.

God begins in 1:1, "The Revelation of Jesus Christ, which God gave unto him, to shew unto his servants' things which must *shortly* come to pass..." 'Shortly' can be defined as '...quickly or swiftly...'" Contrasted to man's varied perceptions of time, God reveals, as Job states in 7:6, "My days are swifter than a weaver's shuttle..." With this understanding firmly in mind, one can only wonder at the speed of '... (These) things which must *shortly* come to pass..." {KJV}

Intrigue thickens as one finishes Job's declaration, "My days are swifter than a weaver's shuttle, *and are spent without hope*." Surely, the lack of 'hope' must be a condemning. One can hear the doubters cry. A fair response would be, 'Understood, but what are the odds Job would decry the loss of hope then, while Paul reveals the *mystery* of our Blessed Hope?' Job's trial days were spent without hope while our days should be spent anticipating our Blessed Hope! That is quite a reversal of practice!

Job's despair reveals the mystery exposed in Romans 15:13, hope/anticipation. Job's Hebrew for 'hope': *tikvah : expectancy – what I long for – could easily be rendered 'anticipation.' Not coincidentally, 'Tikvah' is Israel's national anthem.*

Rev. 1:7 unveils a combination of earlier scriptural passages, Old Testament and New, clarifying Jesus' return to the earth, "Look! He is coming with the clouds, and every eye will see Him, including those who pierced Him. And all the families of the earth will mourn over Him. This is certain. Amen." Chillingly, the Lord emphasizes that the mourning prophesied is inescapable. And all the population of the earth shall mourn! {HCSB}

In verses 10-20, John witnesses Jesus as the Lord in His full Glory, prophesying in a great voice, as of a trumpet. This insight draws us back in contemplation to I Thess. 4:16, giving pause as the similarity of phrasing demands those clarifying details. Now His Bride shall be at His side, He will return to the earth itself, He shall reap judgment on all who have opposed Him.

Jesus proclaims Himself to be the Alpha & Omega, as in the first and the last letters of the Greek alphabet. Displaying His entirety, Jesus, as proclaimed in John 1:1, confirms He is not only the Word, but He is each and every letter, from the first jot to the last tittle. And from this commanding position Jesus instructs the apostle to write letters to the seven Churches in Asia. {ESV}

His amplified voice is described in Rev. 1:15, *"15 His feet were like glowing bronze refined in a furnace. His voice was like the sound of raging waters."* Immediately one is reminded of Paul's Thessalonian description of the Lord descending with a shout, with the voice of an archangel and the trump of God. This time, however, the Lord is appearing to a lone preacher banished to an island prison for his faithfulness to witness of His Lord. {GWT}

I–Ephesus

Jesus then dictates to John the following letters to these seven churches in Asia Minor. First to be communicated with is Ephesus. This congregation is warned to repent and return to its first love or Jesus will come *quickly* and remove its lampstand.

This command cannot be passed over lightly. Paul teaches love never fails. Our first love should be Jesus. Paul declared it was the love of God that compelled him to serve, enumerating the why and wherefore. *"For Christ's love compels us, because we are convinced that one died for all, and therefore all died."* {II Cor. 5:14, NIV}

Jesus has already established the lampstands are the churches receiving the letters. The word here indicates if the congregation does not repent and return to its first love Jesus will come quickly and remove the congregation. {1:20, ESV}

Once again the reader sees a thief in action. Jesus said He would build His church. Now He inadvertently reminds that He can and will remove His Bride quickly, though the reference to removal is negative and not positive in this case.

II–Smyrna

Smyrna is commended for serving God in tribulation and poverty. Instructed not to be afraid, they are promised those faithful that are persecuted unto death will receive the crown of life. This is of course **the same crown of life** referred to also in James 1:12, bestowed upon "those who persevere under trials."

III–Pergamos

Pergamos dwells where Satan's throne sits. Some are faithful in that congregation, yet there are those who hold the doctrine of Balaam, eating things sacrificed to idols and committing sexual immorality. Jesus pleads they repent lest He come quickly and fight against those who hold the doctrine of the Nicolaitans, those who subdue the people, with the sword of His mouth. Jesus performs this warning verbatim in Rev. 19:15, upon His return to the earth at the end of the Tribulation.

IV-Thyatira

Thyatira, 2:25-27, is given the challenge to "...hold fast what you have till I come... And he who overcomes, and keeps My works until the end, to him I will give power over the nations...He shall rule them with a rod of iron; they shall be dashed to pieces like the potter's vessels..." {NKJV}

This encouragement again reminds of James 1:12, "Blessed is the man that endureth temptation: for when he is tried, he shall receive the crown of life, *which the Lord has promised to them that love Him.*" {KJV}

V-Sardis

Sardis receives at once a condemnation and promise of hope. First they are pronounced dead, though they claim life. Then they are encouraged to strengthen that which remains. They are called to remembrance of '...what they've received and heard; to hold fast and repent." Jesus warns them to hold fast and repent lest He come upon them as a thief. Again, the warning of the coming thief.

And in 3:2-3: "Be watchful, and strengthen the things which remain, that are ready to die, for I have not found your works perfect before God. Remember therefore how you have received and heard; hold fast and repent. Therefore, if you will not watch, I will come upon you as a thief, and you will not know what hour I will come upon you." {NKJV}

Once again, Jesus issues the command to be watchful coupled with a warning, "…Therefore if you will not watch, I will come upon you as a thief, and you will not know what hour I will come upon you." Again, as in the Gospels, I Thessalonians, II Peter and here at the last, in Revelation, the prospect of Jesus returning as a thief in the night is preached to those who would be inattentive to His promise, and/or those practicing sin. Certainly, a thief breaks in at any unexpected moment. Talk about an 'inconvenient truth.'

Most importantly, Jesus turns our attention not to the day, but to the hour! Enough said here.

Yet, even in Sardis, Jesus points to those few names that are undefiled and shall '…walk with Me in white, for they are worthy…" This promise hearkens back to Luke 21:36, "Watch ye therefore, and pray always, that ye may be accounted worthy to escape all these things that shall come to pass, and to stand before the Son of man." {KJV}

VI-Philadelphia

Philadelphia is the faithful Church. Philadelphia receives directly the certain prophecy of deliverance by imminent Rapture. But why would this congregation receive such an honor? What would have made these Christians so special to receive a personal promise from Jesus Himself that they would be delivered out of the wrath to come upon the whole earth?

Certainly, Philadelphia had persevered and so won the honor of this astounding deliverance. But *how* had they been able to persevere? The answer is given in their name. Philadelphia is the church of 'Brotherly Love.'

The big fisherman had learned the answer firsthand from Jesus. He confirmed it in I Peter 4:8, "Above all, love each other deeply, because love covers over a multitude of sins." I Cor. 13:8, "Love never fails." {NIV}

Positively one of the most enlightening and encouraging proclamations of the imminent Rapture unfolds here in Rev. 3:10-13:

> *"Because you have kept My command to persevere, I also will keep you from the hour of trial which shall come upon the whole world, to test those who dwell on the earth. Behold, I am coming quickly! Hold fast what you have, that no one may take your crown. He who overcomes, I will make him a pillar in the temple of My God, and he shall go out no more. I will write on him the name of My God and the name of the city of My God, the New Jerusalem, which comes down out of heaven from My God. And I will write on him My new name. He who has an ear, let him hear what the Spirit says to the churches." {NKJV}*

Unquestionably a rich passage on the imminence. Note first, Jesus' multiple commands in the Gospels for us to watch. Invariably, the question arises, "How much?" "Persevere," is the answer. This is not like watching a boring movie. Rather this is like being cast as a principal in a cliff-hanger with a cast of millions! Each day on the set is more amazing than the day before and multitudes across the planet shall literally be the rising stars!

So, let us unpack this rich Philadelphian passage. First, "Because you have kept My command to persevere, I also will keep you from the hour of trial which shall come upon the whole world, to test those who dwell on the earth."

Jesus has continually encouraged his followers in these letters to persevere, observing all that He has commanded. He has said to **watch**, it is a command. He has said to **repent**, it is a command. He has said to **anticipate**, it is a command. The obedient shall be rewarded by being kept '*from the hour of trial which shall come upon the whole world.*'

But how shall faithful believers be kept from the hour of trial coming upon the whole world?

The original word for 'from' in the Greek is 'ek,' which translates as 'out of.' Believers shall be kept **out of** the 'hour' when the Tribulation comes upon the whole earth. How? The process is of course the imminent, ecstatic snatching away of His Bride by Jesus Himself.

Verse 3:11 follows immediately with His most potent promise concerning this event, "Behold, I am coming quickly! Hold fast what you have, that no one may take your crown." Again, Jesus says **quickly**! He commands us to hold fast! Hold fast that no one may *take your crown!* {NKJV}

Paul's prophecy to Timothy concerning the crown of righteousness now jumps off the page! You cannot lose your salvation! But you can lose your rewards! Your crown can be taken from you by enticement into sin! Shockingly, it can be taken at the very last moment!

But take heart! His way of escape is firstly your anticipation of His calling out! He shall shout at any moment in this hour within this time called 'today.'

The entire world is unmindfully approaching a seven-year period of universal catastrophe, suffering war, famine and subjugation unparalleled in all of human history, a time of tribulation that shall never again throughout eternity be equaled! To quote Jesus no less, in Matt. 24:21, **"For then shall be great tribulation, such as was not since the beginning of the world to this time, no, <u>nor ever shall be.</u>"** {KJV}

"While people are saying, 'There is peace and security,' then sudden destruction will come upon them as labor pains come upon a pregnant woman, and they will not escape." {I Thess. 5:3, ESV}

Why do you think the warning that this event will transpire 'quickly' is so oft repeated? Because the event is imminent. It is going to erupt at any moment in a day called 'today'. It cannot be proclaimed too often that the Rapture precedes universal a) disaster, b) world war, c) famine d) plagues, over 'the whole earth.'

Starkly, the attentive are assured emphatically the unmindful '…**will not escape**.' All of this for those who have ears to hear.

Believers are adjured to 'hold fast.' Ever rode 'the Texas Giant' rollercoaster? You have to hang on with all you've got! This is an example of the daily convolutions exponentially multiplying across the earth. Yet Jesus promises all who follow him to receive comfort and strength for each day!

Thus, this admonition is not just to survive in this temporal world. Others are trying to take your eternal crown! We have no idea what all goes with the crown, we only know Kings wear crowns and are the ultimate rulers in their land. Hold fast!

Plus, the overcomer will be made a pillar in the temple of God that shall go out no more. There is divine eternal stability in this gift. Also given to the victor are tattoos of the name of God, the New Jerusalem, and God's new name. You cannot see these gifts now, so God implores you to listen up! He is making this prophecy for all the churches and for all 'whosoever' will!

VII-Laodicea

In God's final letter to the seventh church we discover a mirror image of some modern congregations, especially in America.

Importantly, John again emphasizes the message is being delivered from Jesus Himself. Rev. 3:14, "Write to the angel of the church in Laodicea: "The Amen, the faithful and true Witness, the Originator of God's creation says..." {HCSB}

Jesus reveals Laodicean believers consider themselves rich, wealthy and in need of nothing. He assures them they are instead wretched, miserable, poor, blind and naked.

Coffers in multitudes of church treasuries today are overflowing.

Denominational headquarters buildings are routinely designed plush. Jetting about the world to field outreaches to millions, organizations are seemingly plump and fit. Yet, moral decline is not merely growing, but overwhelming civilization on every level in degradation. Babies are aborted yearly across the globe, over 60 million to date in America alone since Roe v. Wade, Jan. 22nd, 1973.

Presently in the most prosperous country in history, American jails are

woefully inadequate to the tidal wave of new criminals being brought daily to justice.

Jesus' gracious call to repentance to Laodicea echoes down through the millennia to this last-day generation, Rev. 3:20:

"Behold, I stand at the door and knock. If anyone hears my voice and opens the door, I will come in to him and eat with him, and he with me." {ESV}

First, my wife rightly observed, this is Jesus' personal, veiled invitation to the Wedding Supper of the Lamb!

Next, God's call to repent, turn from your sin, and receive His eternal forgiveness and friendship is given here. For skeptics, this identical invitation is repeated at the end of the Bible, in the last chapter of this book of Revelation, 22, with the Lord, His Bride and the Holy Spirit pleading with all who will hear to 'Come!' Get the message?

And with these promises the reader receives another glimpse of the Rapture. John then testifies in Rev. 4:1, "After these things I looked, and behold, a door standing open in heaven. ***And the first voice which I heard was like a trumpet speaking with me***, saying, 'Come up here, and I will show you things which must take place after this." {NKJV}

Jesus has been giving John messages for the churches, but now John is brought into the action of future history. John looks up and sees a door standing open in heaven. Then he hears a voice like a trumpet speaking to him.

We recall Paul's I Thess. 4:16 prophecy. "For the Lord Himself will descend from heaven with a cry of command, with the voice of an archangel, and with the sound of the trumpet of God. And the dead in Christ will rise first." {ESV}

A favorite Bible school teacher, Mr. Marshall Dyches of Tennessee Temple, often intoned the observation, "Remember, repetition is God's theological mucilage." Lest we tire of seeing verses repeated, it is for our mutual learning, as the Holy Spirit gently implants Divine wisdom into our hearts, souls and minds with His Divine glue!

Bringing this passage together with the just quoted Revelation verse discloses God speaking with an angelic voice like a trumpet. That's the sound!

"Come up here..." begins the command. Where? Into heaven. God is going to reveal to John future events that 'must' take place 'after this.' This is prophecy, folks! God is preaching what is going to be!

Deep within the book of Revelation, after many exposures to the future events that will flood the Tribulation, God parenthetically issues another warning in chapter 16, verse 15, "**Behold, I come as a thief. Blessed *is* he that watcheth, and keepeth his garments, lest he walk naked, and they see his shame. {KJV}**

This warning, again with God coming as a thief, might appear to some as redundancy, but God never, ever communicates superfluously. In this warning, God ushers the reader into the very reality of the end times, the days Jesus likened unto the days of Noah. The consistency of these prophecies and warnings also corroborate God's faithfulness to truth.

For years into centuries past, man has wondered how total depravity could be described. This was of course, before the internet and the promulgation of pornography, daily murders and worse sin. This writer gratefully cannot imagine to what degree this assault on civilization will have reached in the days following the publication of this work and then following up to Jesus' return to the earth. One can only say that there is no difficulty in understanding Jesus' warning to 'watch' and 'keep his garments, lest he walk naked, and they see his shame.'

Enfolded into Chapter 21:9-10 rests another glimpse into the placement of the Rapture as pre-Tribulation. John is offered a glimpse of the Bride, to which he gladly agrees. John is whisked away to the New Jerusalem "... descending out of heaven..." where John meets Jesus, the Holy Spirit, and the Bride, who together, continue to plead for all who will to "come."

Recall that Chapter 19:7 reveals the marriage of the Lamb, **and the wife has made herself ready!** Then Jesus returns to the earth! However, God's Word closes in Chapter 22 with the Bride in the New Jerusalem! New wives are commonly referred to as the blushing Bride.

The last chapter of Revelation includes the terrifying admonition for all remaining on the earth to continue in their station. Rev. 22:11, "Let the one who does wrong continue to do wrong; let the vile person continue to be vile; let the one who does right continue to do right; and let the holy person continue to be holy." {NIV}

This declaration to continue and allow sin to flourish alongside righteousness returns the student of scripture to Romans 1:26, "For this cause God gave them up unto vile affections: for even their women did change the natural use into that which is against nature..." {KJV}

It is no mystery now why John would have been inspired to encourage believers to anticipate the Rapture in I John 3:3, explaining that those who practiced this anticipation would at once also be purifying themselves, even as Jesus is pure.

God's emphatic warning cannot be glossed over at the very end of this last and final God-breathed book of Revelation. Jesus declares once more with finality in Rev. 22:20, "He who testifies to these things says, *"Surely I am coming quickly."* {NKJV}

And thus, the response of those reading the book, of those believers watching the signs of the end times exponentially multiplying, listening for God's shout of deliverance absolutely must be, *"Amen. Even so, come, Lord Jesus!"*

But the last and final word given by God, Rev. 22:21, is a comfort, blessing, and also an instruction, "The grace of our Lord Jesus Christ be with you all. Amen." {NKJV}

How are believers to be found at the Shout, in that moment, that twinkling of an eye? They are to be found in His Grace, one and all. Prayerfully, unashamedly, with eager anticipation. Amen.

You may now nudge your fellow believers around you, if you are reading this on a tablet, or your iPhone or some such electronic device, or to the shrinking few readers perusing this in an actual book! Unless you are blind you should be seeing the Day approaching. You might want to begin to consider the hour.

Denominations have been built around the end times and His Return. Some have been built on His not returning. Standing in the middle of the stream of knowledge, planted as a signpost for the ages, Revelation,

Chapter 22:20, boasts one of the plainest statements of the doctrine of Jesus' imminent Rapture.

Encompassing the teaching of the Rapture within the promise of His Return, Jesus proclaims, "Surely, I come quickly!" Even at the close of the Bible, Jesus imparts one more declaration to His calling out.

These truths fairly scream at the reader from the final pages of Holy Writ.

John is in the midst of being given a magnificent tour de force of the New Jerusalem by one of the seven angels who had just dispensed judgment vials of the seven last plagues across the earth. Afterwards this angel had been dispatched to John in Rev. 21:9, with the invitation, "Come hither, I will shew thee the bride, the Lamb's wife." {KJV}

Remember, in the opening of Revelation 4:1, John had been taken up into Heaven to be shown the things that '...must be hereafter.' John is now being escorted into the reality of the future present. To lead John to the Bride, the angel first reveals the city of God, which is where the Bride lives. And, now, as Chapter 22 opens, John is in the city of God, and being instructed by the angel on how things are going to be in this glorious realm.

In verse six, John notes the angel explains, "And he said unto me, 'These sayings *are* faithful and true.' And the Lord God of the holy prophets sent his angel to shew unto his servants the things *which must shortly be done*." (KJV)

God is outside of time. He directs His servants in time to guide those who follow Him through the ages to the beyond. The angel here emphasizes these things, '... must shortly be done."

Immediately, God interjects in 22:7, "...Behold, I come quickly: blessed is he that keepeth the sayings of the prophecy of this book." {KJV}

The Bible study you are receiving here is focusing on the singular prophecy of the imminent Rapture. And now, Jesus, in this close of Revelation once again emphasizes that He is coming quickly! In a moment, in the twinkling of an eye, while it is still called 'today.' The apostle John has already written that those who hold the anticipation of this event consciously purify themselves even as Jesus is pure. Jesus is coming quickly, and His followers are to be watching for and anticipating this event!

For all who fear an overt exaggeration of this antici-pation, the angel in verse 10 proclaims, "...Do not seal the words of the prophecy of this book, for the time is at hand." {NKJV}

Immediately the reader is transported back to Daniel 12:4, *"But thou, O Daniel, shut up the words, and seal the book, even to the time of the end: many shall run to and fro, and knowledge shall be increased."* {KJV}

Yes, Daniel was commanded to keep the prophecies of the end of time sealed. Lest any be tempted to unseal the book prematurely. The reason God commanded the book be sealed is because these specific prophecies of Daniel were designated for the end of the age. Always faithful to His Word, God now commands the angel here to order John **_not_** to seal the words of the prophecy of the book of Revelation. This is the time to preach His Return is at hand!

One is instantaneously confronted with Paul's I Cor. 7:29 admonition, "But this I say, brethren, the time has been shortened, so that from now on..." God had quick-ened Paul decades before Revelation was given that

God was shortening the times. Believer perspective was honed from that point to be viewed as "…from now on…" {NASB}

To avoid putting the cart before the horse, Jesus will Rapture His Bride out of the world before His wrath descends!

The reason for this command? Because the time is near! It's not 3,000 years hence from the exposure to these prophecies. It is instead '*near*.'

Believers are commanded to tell the world of the prophecies of this book. Israel is back in the land. Hostility is growing across the planet for the children of God. In fact, hostility is exploding between the nations. Wars, rumors of wars, earthquakes, hurricanes, pestilences, perplexity of nations, carousing's, and violence across the earth are manifesting exponentially.

Jesus is at the door. He has testified He is coming back. He has stated these things must shortly come to pass.

To underline this truth, Jesus comforts his sheep with the encouragement that He is coming back *quickly*, in a moment, in the twinkling of an eye! He declares this truth three times in this final chapter and word of the Bible:

*"**Behold I come quickly**!"* {Rev. 22:7, 12, & 20; KJV}

(This is Jesus preaching, folks!)

To believers this is the greatest of encouragements. To those who do not know Jesus this is intended to be the most terrible of warnings.

And John responds, "Even so, come Lord Jesus!"

{Rev. 22:20, NKJV}

John could have responded immediately, "Amen." But Jesus had one more Blessing to bestow on His Bride through John.

Any moment now, while it is called 'today,' He shall descend to the clouds and Shout! And instantaneously, in an atom-smashing moment, inside the twinkling of an eye, within the environs of 11/100ᵗʰ's of a second, we, His Bride, will ***blast off*** this earth in the greatest ride anyone, anytime, anywhere has ever experienced!

The countdown began in eternity past, before the foundation of the world, and now is exponentially rushing

Down
To meet
Us!!!

"Let not your heart be troubled." {John 14:1}

And so, God's Word finishes first

In blessing,
followed by
closing with
His inspired Confirmation:

" *"The Grace of Our Lord Jesus Christ
be with you all.*
Amen."
{Rev. 22:21, NKJV}

Afterword

Rapiemur

{The Eloping moment of the Bride with Jesus}

"deinde nos qui vivimus qui relinquimur simul rapiemur cum illis in nubibus obviam Domino in aera et sic semper cum Domino erimus" {I Thess. 4:17, (Latin Vulgate Bible), LXX}

"Then we who are alive, who are left, shall be <u>taken up</u> together with them in the clouds to meet Christ, into the air: and so shall we be always with the Lord." {I Thess. 4:17, (English, LV), LXX}

"…caught up…" {KJV}
Here rendered "… taken up …" {LXX}
From Jerome's Latin Vulgate – rapiemur:
in English – translation:
'snatched with ecstasy'…

"rapiemur,"

205

Latin-English Dictionary online:
Translation // English:
first-person plural future passive indicative of **rapiō**
"we shall be snatched, we shall be grabbed,
we shall be carried off"

*"The word 'rapture' (caught up physically **and in ecstasy**) has come into popular use today to refer to the Lord Jesus' coming for His Bride (the church), to lift her up into the heavens (v. 17). It derives from the word 'rapio' in the Latin Bible's translation of this verse. One raptured is **'lifted up' in love."** (The Christian Life Bible, the Christian Life Master Outlines and Study Notes–Group XI. The Last Days: Master Outline #49–The Four Phases of the Second Coming, "The Rapture of the Church.") {1 Thessalonians 4:13-18, page 1211}*

Epilogue

To: the Skeptics, Naysayers, Deniers, Gainsayers
& Especially the Loyal Opposition of The Imminent
Rapture.

As pointed out in this book, and previously by such astute prophetical scholars as the deservedly esteemed, and now divinely glorified former American Dean of Bible Prophecy, Dr. John F. Walvoord, the number of those in Christendom who gainsay the teaching of the Rapture is in the majority and growing, might one suggest 'exponentially,' even day by day, and moment by moment.

The adopted attitude of the majority of many of those professing belief in the imminent Rapture is *laissez faire* (... an attitude of letting things take their own course, without interfering ...)

Included are many of the recognized scholarly, exemplified by the testimony of the learned professor at the beginning of this book, who find it difficult to publicly proclaim they believe in the imminent Rapture.

In fact, yours truly, who has piloted this Fourth Edition of 'Blast Off' to landing, has not forgotten the initial work, devoted to this prophecy, *When Now Becomes Too Late*.

Leading up to that publication, my personal surprise registered profoundly at the discovery of my own blatant intimidation to publishing a manuscript supporting my personal belief in the imminent, pre-millennial, pre-Tribulation Rapture.

This fear materialized as the work approached completion. The question emblazoned itself across my psyche, "Do you really want to publish a book that proclaims to the world that you believe at any moment, on a day that *must* be called 'today', Jesus is going to snatch you and every other Christian, dead and alive, out of this world before the Tribulation begins?"

It had been easy to declare in private discussions. It was even simple to preach from the pulpit, regardless of the size of the congregation. But going public, compounded by the fact that the potential audience is the world, becomes daunting on a whole new level. Example: #gone!

However, it was this realization that brought me to recognize the ease with which all of us carry ideas without ever testing their reality. It was the Word of God, studied in prayerful submission that convinced me this teaching is true and therefore demanded promulgation. And, finally, it was the gathering of support through scholarship that convinced me many others could benefit from publishing the Bible's straight forward proclamation of the imminent Rapture.

Of first concern was the multitude of billions on earth unaware of this teaching. Interest was sharpened by the tens of millions of Christians rejecting this doctrine. But encouragement was stirred by recognizing the many believers desiring support for their acceptance of the imminent Rapture teaching.

Jesus said, "Go therefore and make disciples of all nations, baptizing them in the name of the Father and of the Son and of the Holy Spirit, teaching them to observe **all that I have commanded you**. And behold, I am with you always, to the end of the age." {Matt. 28:19-20, ESV}

There it was again. "...the end of the age..." was not something to ignore. The nations of the world were the target audience. Paul completed the equation with, "As we have therefore opportunity, let us do good unto *all men, especially* unto them who are of the household of faith." We should minister *especially* to the household of faith! *That means preaching to the choir!* {Gal. 6:10, KJV}

All of these realizations culminating together drew me on to complete the first book.

It was at this crossroads of greater understandings that my personal testimony infiltrated the command decision to publish and make public to the world my personal view of the imminent, any moment Shout of Jesus on a day that must be called 'today.'

As the Pendulum Swings

Roughly <u>20 years ago</u> I began writing what would become my first ever book of any kind, this one on the prophecy of our Blessed Hope, the Rapture, with just a working title to aid in keeping the focus of the topic central to the theme.

Following is a brief testimony of how God confirmed the propriety of my view and accuracy of that focused 'working title' itself:

How short is the time before Jesus Shouts ...?

In preparing to publish what would become a book on the imminent, any moment Rapture, I suffered pause. Although the temporary 'working title' I had employed to frame the work had well-served its' purpose, approaching publication for real, I became fearful the working title, *When Now Becomes Too Late*, was too pushy, too 'in your face,' to use as the actual, proper title to introduce my perspective on the next major prophetical, Biblical event Scripturally slated to erupt on planet earth.

Start to finish, from the conception of the topic to the final draft, the writing had dominated the last 2-3 years of my and my family's lives.

I was preparing to take a giant leap of faith from a cliff whose base was shrouded somewhere below the mists I was pondering.

So, killing two birds with one stone, I took the family to vacate in Corpus Christi, to the beach, and to pray and seek God's leading on the title. It was my first profes-sional submission after all, and I was naturally anxious for multiple reasons.

Overlooking the Gulf of Mexico, we had a great time, but prayer and seeking God's direction seemed vain.

Apparently no answer was forthcoming from God.

Going to the lobby to sign out the last day, was sur-prised to find the smallish hall filled with folks watching large tv monitors scattered around. It looked like a good movie, but I was trying to get outta there. Went to the desk and found the young clerk with his back to the public, watching the same film on his screen.

Trying to grab his attention, I prodded, "Must be a great movie?" "Not a movie, a news report," he countered, not turning around.

The clerk, appearing to be young and inexperienced, was firm in his assessment.

Having been a military journalist, followed by stints acting on stage and in films, and having lived in NYC, the obvious location of this movie, and above all, anxious to get signed out, I swung my arm back toward the lobby trying to gain his attention by correcting him when I spun back around to him exclaiming, "The other tower just collapsed!"

Now turning to me, he explained, "Sir, I'm trying to tell you. This is a news report. This is happening in New York City right now, this morning," he emphasized, staring directly into my eyes while studying my face for reaction.

We watched in silence over the next few moments as first one tower would collapse and then the other.

I then knew my prayers had been answered, because the working title I had feared was too 'in your face' was being confirmed for publication to the world as a bullseye. I realized with my background in journalism and Show Business, if I'd had the wherewithal at that moment, I could be reading my book to the world on television from the streets of lower Manhattan.

Standing there watching the towers collapsing over and over again, the 'working' title I'd been hesitating to make official, and fervently, fearfully praying about, continued to flash through my mind: *"When Now Becomes Too Late"**

I also knew that with the publication process, to some in the aftermath of this disaster, I'd be an 'also-ran' at best, or an 'ambulance chaser' in the worst. Yet the title had been formed for focus early in the beginning of writing the book several years before.

Then began the battle to decide how to deal with this international disaster linked so formidably by timing with my book's title. Should there be a re-titling? Perhaps a re-write, to include the disaster? How?

Over the next couple months as I mothered the myriad of publication details to a finish, I decided to mention it only briefly.

https://www.youtube.com/watch?v=O0hlPBnC_q0

*An early editorial review compared this first work, '*WNBTL*', as a cross between C.S. Lewis' 'Mere Christianity' and Sun-Tzu's 'The Art of War.' I did not then foresee the soon move to publish a second book, *Distant Reaches, an* autobiographical adventure of my early days leading to conversion to Jesus and Christianity. That writing became an effort to introduce myself to the publishing world and beyond. Thus was the circumspection befalling me as I re-entered the multi-faceted glass world of media.

Certainly, even more amazing was the overwhelming involvement I found myself in over the following years working on a second, more extensively detailed study of the imminence of our Blessed Hope, which itself has in fact spawned further editions, now in progress to becoming the Fourth Edition, " *Blast Off Rapiemur – Jesus Himself Speaks to the Rapture.*"

Leading Rapture Challenges

The 'Rapture' challenges proffered by the loyal opposition can be minimized to Four primary questions of scholarship:

1) Is the teaching of the imminent Rapture truly honored by Scripture?
2) Moreover, did the early Church teach and practice belief in the imminent Rapture?
3) How important is the proclamation of the imminent Rapture?
4) Why did God schedule the 'imminence' when He knew the moment, hour and day of Jesus' Shout?

Anyone disparaging or diminishing this last key point of doctrine is left with a bucket of additional embarrassing questions to which one must either agree or deny the faith once delivered unto the saints. To quote once again, Jesus' half-brother Jude, "Beloved, although I was very eager to write to you about our common salvation, I found it necessary to write appealing to you to contend for the faith that was once for all delivered to the saints." {Jude verse 3, ESV}{Author's note: Also read *Jude*, GW}

1)
The Imminent Rapture – Scripture Based ?

Scriptural support of this paramount prophecy is overwhelmingly apparent, as per the myriad of examples provided in this manuscript. In fact, the passages considered in this work confirm unequivocally that recognition of any ignorance of this element of Christian faith causes an eruption of alarming astonishment to we believers who are alive and remain, eagerly awaiting the Shout. We shall therefore strive to avoid straying from the path of the four suggested, representative and primary concerns demanded by the loyal opposition.

Read first the epistle of Jude for his confession of being '***very eager***' to write believers in Jesus, known first as Christians in Antioch, ostensibly to address their understanding of salvation, only to be compelled by the Holy Spirit, {II Tim. 3:16}, to abruptly change course and plead rather for their contending 'for the faith once delivered to the saints.'

Place this eagerness alongside the multiple entreaties given by Paul throughout His epistles commending individual Christians and even entire congregations of followers of Jesus Christ for their public eagerness in watching and waiting for the Lord's Shout for His Bride. Eagerness resulting from receiving the 'faith' to accept the teaching of her imminent catching away.

These entreaties following on the heels of Jesus' continual, multiple warnings to be ready at any hour of the day or night for His saving intervention.

So, we can safely declare Scripture profoundly proclaims the doctrine of the imminent Rapture of the Church on a day that MUST be called 'today'!

2)
The Imminent Rapture – Early Church Didactic ?

Opposing the concept of political correctness, Jude vies for contention, if one may risk redundancy.

Some Christians, in struggling with the volatile subject of the imminent Rapture, a challenging prophecy to be sure, have submitted themselves to a position of rendering the teaching to a lesson of childish splendor. They position their perspective to an innocence of, "Jesus is going to return whenever He wants, so we don't have to worry our pretty little heads about it."

If this were the proper attitude to adopt, then Jesus' imperative commands to watch as the events of the end times begin to coalesce would be pointless. His further encouragement to be prepared to escape all the trials that are going to befall the earth in Luke 21:36, added to His imperative commands to watch, would be nonsensical.

Paul's closing of Chapter Four, verse 18, of I Thess., his instruction for believers to comfort one another with this promise would be meaningless tripe. And the Apostle's added commendation in the following chapter to believers that are strengthening one another with this message of the imminent Rapture would be in the very least curious for its inclusion. {I Thess. 5:11}

Paul's numerous commendations to various believers and local churches for their eager observance of this watch for His calling out would also be absurd, not to mention pointedly bankrupt.

All of these points, throughout the New Testament, taken en masse, scream with divine purpose to the spiritually blind and deaf that the proclamation of the imminent Rapture was *indeed* New Testament, first century doctrine and practice!

In short, yes, the early Church did teach the imminent Rapture.

3)
The Imminent Rapture – Divine Proclamation ?

To ascribe the initial teaching of this key prophecy to the likes of the 18th century's John Darby or more recent proclaimers merely reveals the ignorance of those bereft of any solid Biblical scholarship. Sadly, many folks take the word of someone else rather than do any Berean digging themselves.

Avoiding dissertation on doctrinal positions over the centuries to redeem the time, one only has to confirm Matthew Henry's view of this issue from his personal commentaries, gathering dust on the shelves of the aforementioned scoffers. Henry was after all extant over a century before Darby.

Most devastatingly, once the reality of the divine inspiration and authority of Holy Scripture soaks in, the contention that the teaching of the imminent Rapture, or any part of the doctrine is contrived, is embarrassingly laughable. First Century church position is clearly established in the preceding chapters of this work alone to suffice the stand that establishes the imminent Rapture on solid Scriptural ground.

Documentation has been supplied for the two centuries leading up to Darby's Day by Dr. William C. Watson, in his wonderful compendium of pre-Darby proclamations in his work, "Dispensationalism Before Darby." (See my Amazon review following ☺)

God's Timing

'Dispensationalism Before Darby'
By Dr. William C. Watson
December 24, 2015

Dispensationalism deals with God's timing of events in the world. Author Dr. William C. Watson's work, ergo, refines the order upon which man's perception of God's timeline was advancing in the two centuries before John

Nelson Darby. (Focusing on the doctrine of the imminence of the Rapture.-author's note)

Darby is the man erroneously credited by others, not himself, with initiating the teaching of the imminent, or any moment, Rapture.

"Dispensationalism Before Darby" provides a crucial compendium of documented 17th and 18th century sources to immolate the proposed error that 19th Century Darby was responsible for concocting the imminent Rapture doctrine.

Establishing a veritable literary fusillade of testimony supporting the teaching of the imminent Rapture doctrine during the 17th and 18th centuries, obviously pre-dating John Nelson Darby, this weighty tome offers hours of detailed, pleasurable reading for all concerned.

Truly, Nelson is credited with formulating "classical dispensationalism" by scholars such as Dr. Ed Hindson, Dean & Distinguished Professor of Religion, School of Religion, Liberty University.

Pointedly, however, Hindson declares, "...Watson plows new ground in researching the history of eschatological thought prior to the nineteenth century."

Certainly, some few Bible Scholars familiar with Matthew Henry, publishing his famed commentary a century before Darby, are aware that Henry's commentary records his own support of the imminent Rapture stance. Strangely, most of those allowing Henry's commentary to gather dust on their overladen library shelves are not.

Thus, importantly, this volume eradicates the claim that Darby inspired the teaching.

Significantly, this line of thought is highlighted when one considers the Rapture as viewed by all of these witnesses from the centuries leading up to Darby, at that earlier date proclaimed popularly by Biblical scholars as 'imminent'!

For the initial proclamations of the imminent Rapture in the 1st century Church, you are referred to "Blast Off Rapiemur."

Well done, Dr. Watson !!!

Till the Shout!

TL Farley,
author,
Blast Off Rapiemur – the 1st century proclamation of the Imminent Rapture. I Thess. 4:17

Once more then, even more profound, the preaching of our Blessed Hope was wonderfully documented by apostles of the first-generation church, with congregations in lively practice of the belief, in the first century, as attested to heavily in these pages.

The most striking support for the teaching of the imminent Rapture is initiated by the least of the Apostles, Paul himself, to the Thessalonian congregation:

> *"For since we believe that Jesus died and rose again, even so, through Jesus, God will bring with him those who have fallen asleep." {I Thess. 4:14, ESV}*

As Paul introduces the teaching of the imminent Rapture to the Thessalonicans in this most famous and illustrative passage of the 'snatching' away of the Bride of Christ by Jesus Himself, God inspires the self-proclaimed 'least of the apostles' to bedrock the teaching upon the Resurrection itself! Within a decade Paul underlines the same connection while familiarizing the Corinthians on the practice of the Lord's Supper.

Paul plants the authority of his teaching of the imminent Rapture on the foundation of the death, burial and resurrection of Jesus Christ! Paul founds the promise of the Rapture on the very Gospel!! {I Thess. 4:14}

Parenthetically, greetings on Resurrection Sunday, popularized over the recent past centuries as 'Easter,' which begs its own discussion, should obviously be "Maranatha!"

All of this shall become transparent at the very first lurch of the Greatest Ride off Earth!!!

And all believers, dead and alive shall experience collectively and personally their initial jolt of Divine Ecstasy!

In verse 17, Paul cements the 'imminent' aspect by emphasizing 'we who are alive and remain shall be 'caught up' (*rapiemur*) with them, the transforming dead. Within a decade plus Paul is awarded his goal of gaining entrance to the first load of Jesus' Shout as a martyr. But his point stays, '… we who are alive and remain…' declares the any moment imminence!

So, finally, the prominence of the teaching of the Rapture is in sync and in fact supported by example with the death, burial and Resurrection of Jesus Christ our Lord!

Yes, the teaching of the imminent Rapture is of first importance!

<u>4)</u>
<u>The Imminent Rapture – God Scheduled?</u>

<u>Knowing the revelation was two millennia hence</u> !

This prophetic mystery might appear to some as a sadistically cruel joke, especially considering the time lapse from Paul's proclamation in I Cor. 15:52 of 'any moment' to this present hour, two millennia later.

Even in Peter's day, some familiar with the Genesis account began to waver and challenge the teaching. {II Peter 3:1-18, NIV-UK}

Yet, examination through God's word exposes the conclusion. As each generation has passed, through each century, in each individual person's life, each new day, each new hour, each new moment bursts with the reality 'be ready !' Scripture affords, the dead in Christ shall rise first, and then we who yet remain shall be caught up, (rapiemur),with them, ever to be with Our Lord !

Our Rapture and deliverance have always been imminent, from before the foundation of the world!

Maranatha Till Blast Off!!!!

20813675
20813675

Dated Scriptural Alignment

The Chapter Headings Were Added in the Thirteenth Century:

A man named Stephen Langton divided the Bible into chapters in the year A.D. 1227.
Langton was a professor at the University of Paris, later elevated to Archbishop of Canterbury.

The Verse Enumerations Were Added in the Sixteenth Century:

Robert Stephanus (Stephens), a French printer, divided the verses for his Greek New Testament.
It was published in 1551.

The First Bible with Chapter And Verse Divisions:

The first entire Bible in which these chapter and verse divisions were used was Stephen's edition of the Latin Vulgate (1555). The first English New Testament to have both chapter and verse divisions was the Geneva Bible (1560). Fortunately, Jewish scholars have followed the way of dividing the Hebrew Scripture into chapters and verses. **(blueletterbible.org)**

Bible Source Reference – Abbreviations

American King James Version – Am-KJV
Aramaic Bible in Plain English – ABPE
Authorized King James Version – Au-KJV
Berean Literal Bible – BLB
Berean Study Bible – BSB
Darby Bible Translation – DBT
English Standard Version – ESV
1599 Geneva Bible - GNV
God's Word Translation – GWT
Holman Christian Standard Bible – HCSB
International Standard Version – ISV
Jubilee Bible 2000 – JB2
King James 2000 – KJ2
King James Version – KJV
Latin Vulgate – LXX
NET Bible – NET
New American Standard Bible (1977) – NASB
New International Version – NIV
New International Version-UK – NIV-UK
New King James Version – NKJV
New Living Translation – NLT
Webster's Bible Translation – WBT
Young's Literal Translation – YLT

Bible Book – Abbreviations

O.T.

Genesis – Gen.
Leviticus – Lev.
Numbers – Num.
II Kings – 2 Kin.
I Chronicles – I Chr.
Job – Job
Psalms – Ps.
Proverbs – Prov.
Ecclesiastes – Eccl.
Isaiah – Is.
Jeremiah – Jer.
Daniel – Dan.
Hosea – Hos.
Micah – Mic.
Zephaniah – Zeph.
Zechariah – Zech.
Malachi – Mal.

N.T.

James – James
I Thessalonians – I Thess.
II Thessalonians – II Thess.
Galatians – Gal.
Matthew – Matt.
Mark – Mark
Luke – Luke
Romans – Rom.
I Corinthians – I Cor.
II Corinthians – II Cor.
I Peter – I Pet.
II Peter – II Pet.
Ephesians – Eph.
Acts – Acts
Colossians – Col.
Philippians – Philip.
Hebrews – Heb.
I Timothy – I Tim.
Titus – Titus
Jude – Jude
II Timothy – II Tim.
I John – I John.
II John – II John.
III John – III John
Revelation – Rev.
Gospel of John – John.

Chronological Book Dating

Tanakh // Old Testament
b.c. 4004 — Genesis
b.c. 1491-1000 — Psalms
b.c. 971-560 — II Kings
b.c. 487 — Zechariah
b.c. 485 — Nehemiah
b.c. 397 — Malachi

Brit Chadashah // New Testament
a.d. 45-50–James
a.d. 51–I Thessalonians
a.d. 51–II Thessalonians
a.d. 52-58–Galatians
a.d. 55-65–Matthew
a.d. 55-65–Mark
a.d. 55-65–Luke
a.d. 55-65 — John
a.d. 57-60–Romans
a.d. 59–I Corinthians
a.d. 60–II Corinthians
a.d. 60-63–I Peter
a.d. 60- 64–II Peter
a.d. 61-64–Ephesians

a.d. 62–Acts
a.d. 63-64–Colossians
a.d. 63-64 Philemon
a.d. 63-64–Philippians
a.d. 64–Hebrews
a.d. 64–I Timothy
a.d. 64-65–Titus
a.d. 66–Jude
a.d. 68–II Timothy
a.d. 90-98–I John
a.d. 90-98–II John
a.d. 90-98–III John
a.d. 96–Revelation

URL Index

answersingenesis.org

biblegateway.com

biblehub.com

blbclassic.org

creationstudies.org

defenderpublishing.com

en.wiktionary.org

www.goodreads.com

hallindsey.com

jackvanimpe.com

latinvulgate.com

masterbooks.net

perseus.tufts.edu

pre-trib.org

quod.lib.umich.edu

wordhippo.com

Scripture Index

Acknowledgments

---

*First and foremost, to my wife, Karen Ann, for her
continuing,* unflagging *support in this ongoing project,
reaching to this Fourth Edition, and most importantly,
encourager in our Lord and Savior, Jesus Christ.
And our boys, Daniel & Samuel, for their gracious
gift of time, and growing interest in the projects,
to allow the demanding focus on this work.*

E *special gratitude & kudos to both* <u>www.biblegateway.</u>
<u>com</u> *&* <u>www.biblehub.com</u> *for their exceedingly gra-
cious and permissive access to their excellent and invaluable sites.* "...Blessed indeed," says the Spirit, "that they
may rest from their labors, for their deeds follow them!"
{Revelation 14:13c, English Standard Version}

And to <u>www.google.com</u>, *without whose cavernous
repository of reference this manuscript would yet be 'a
work in process.'* "And I gave my heart to seek and search
out by wisdom concerning all *things* that are done under
heaven: this sore travail hath God given to the sons of
man to be exercised therewith." {Ecclesiastes 1:13, King
James Version}

Also, <u>www.microsoft.com</u> groups MS Office, Editing
Division; and all of the countless sites across the Internet
that provided the invaluable jots and tittles essential to all

endeavors of scholarship. {King James Version, Proverbs 25:11 – "A word fitly spoken *is like* apples of gold in pictures of silver." & "For truly I tell you, until heaven and earth disappear, not the smallest letter, not the least stroke of a pen, will by any means disappear from the Law until everything is accomplished." {Matthew 5:18, New International Version}

Finally, and most importantly, Xulon Press and Salem Publishing, truly a support for providing Christian authors a platform. From inception: Special thanks to Project Coordinator Jose Medina for his patience, and Brittnee Newman of Editorial for her availability and insight. Also, especially, Chris Gonzalez, Author Support, for corrections. An especial kudo to Katie Tota, Salem Author Representative, for flawless updating assists and Scripture Index support. And much gratitude to SAR Rachel Brown & a very well done to the typesetters, especially rising to the continuing monumental challenges with the Scripture Index corrections. Jason Fletcher, for his unflagging encouragement from the very beginning. And, finally, the Salem Author Rep cadre, especially Jessica Brown. And, most finally and with much gratitude, for the extraordinary, detailed attention to chapter layout. To the praise of His Eternal Glory. Well, well done, Jaci Johnson, After Press Rep. and thank you all.

> { *"The Lord gave the word: great was the company of those that published it." Psalm 68:11, KJV.* }

Other Books by TL Farley:

When Now Becomes Too Late: Microscopes the very moment of Jesus' Shout for His Bride itself, traveling inside the atom-smashing twinkle of the prophecy that has become known as 'the Rapture'.

Distant Reaches: Autobiographical adventures:

1) *The Letter* – International intrigue beginning with my first quaffed Guinness of the day at the Falcon Inn, Portobello, Dublin, Ireland.
2) *In Search of John* – Pushing a hack for Red Cab of Boston, *'yer'* man is commandeered by a hysterical mother in search of her missing son.
3) *The Fishing Trip* – Part I - Hitching south out of Braintree, Mass., in a blinding snowstorm, crossing the George Washington Bridge out of Manhattan, I land work on the Sheila Mae, a fishing boat out of Cape May, New Jersey, only to meet a hurricane face to face 200 miles off the coast of North Carolina. {Ps. 107:23-30; Matt. 4:19; NKJV}

II) Detainment & Interrogation by a New Jersey State Highway Police Detective.
III) Epiphany.

Email: *anymoment@att.net*

Caveat

- A notice, especially in a probate, that certain actions may not be taken without informing the person who gave the notice.

E very effort has been made in polishing this manuscript to ford the middle stream of communication of this present day, here at the beginning of the 21ˢᵗ century.

Taking into consideration the exponential proliferation of media, continuing electronic permutations and the dissolution of formal educational restraints as exemplified in such scholastic pursuits as the "Core" movement, it is acknowledged that this present vantage point reveals a wide vista of interlocking communications.

The incontestable torrent of knowledge flooding the world recalls the 1970's Alvin Toffler title, '*Future Shock*,' which forewarned of the informational tsunami by which we in this present day, nearing five decades later, are now awash.

This same thought was first proclaimed as prophecy 2.5 millennia ago by the Prophet Daniel:

b.c. 534 - "⁴But thou, O Daniel, shut up the words, and seal the book, even to the time of the end:

many shall run to and fro, and knowledge shall be increased." {Daniel 12:4, Au-KJV}

That said, all the best, and good fishing as we seek to continue onward and upward until ...

Jesus Shouts!

CPSIA information can be obtained
at www.ICGtesting.com
Printed in the USA
FSHW011324250320
68463FS